2

ENERGY POLICIES, POLITICS AND PRICES

ENERGY DIVERSITY FOR ECONOMIC PROGRESS

STRATEGY AND ISSUES

ENERGY POLICIES, POLITICS AND PRICES

Additional books in this series can be found on Nova's website under the Series tab.

Additional e-books in this series can be found on Nova's website under the e-book tab.

ENERGY POLICIES, POLITICS AND PRICES

ENERGY DIVERSITY FOR ECONOMIC PROGRESS

STRATEGY AND ISSUES

SIMONE WILLIAMS
EDITOR

NOVINKA

New York

For permission to use material from this book please contact us:
Telephone 631-231-7269; Fax 631-231-8175
Web Site: http://www.novapublishers.com

Library of Congress Cataloging-in-Publication Data

ISBN: 978-1-63321-577-1

Published by Nova Science Publishers, Inc. † New York

Contents

PREFACE

This book discusses the all-of-the-above energy strategy as a path to sustainable economic growth; the reemergence of the U.S. as a global petroleum producer; the issues Congress faces with the energy policy; and provides an overview of unconventional oil and natural gas.

Chapter 1 – The U.S. energy sector is undergoing a profound transformation. The United States is producing more oil and natural gas, is generating more electricity from renewables such as wind and solar, and is consuming less petroleum while holding electricity consumption constant. These developments have had substantial economic and energy security benefits, and they are helping to reduce carbon emissions in the energy sector and thereby tackle the challenge posed by climate change.

To build on this progress, to foster economic growth, and to protect the planet for future generations, the President has set out an aggressive All-of-the-Above strategy on energy. Some of the recent trends in the energy sector predate the Administration and stem from technological advances and risk-taking by American entrepreneurs and businesses, as well as from government-supported research and other public policies. The All-of-the-Above energy strategy supports these trends through environmentally responsible production of oil and natural gas. In addition, the Administration has advanced the growth of energy sources with low or zero carbon emissions through programs that support wind, solar, other renewables, and nuclear, and has also helped to reduce energy demand by promoting energy efficiency. The Administration is also supporting an ambitious program of carbon capture, utilization and storage for coal and natural gas power plants and for industrial facilities.

The All-of-the-Above energy strategy has three key elements: to support economic growth and job creation, to enhance energy security, and to deploy low-carbon energy technologies and lay the foundation for a clean energy future. This report lays out these three elements of the All-ofthe-Above energy strategy, and takes stock of the progress that has been made to date and the work that remains to be done.

Chapter 2 – In May 2013, domestic production of petroleum in the United States surpassed imports for the first time since January 1997. The fact that domestic production has outpaced imports is not some random occurrence, but rather the culmination of trends that have been in motion for a number of years. Imports of petroleum have been declining over the last 7 years, while domestic production has undergone a significant revival. According to a forecast by the International Energy Agency, "The United States will overtake Saudi Arabia to become the world's biggest petroleum producer before 2020, and will be energy independent 10 years later."

Chapter 3 – Energy policy in the United States has focused on three major goals: assuring a secure supply of energy, keeping energy costs low, and protecting the environment. In pursuit of those goals, government programs have been developed to improve the efficiency with which energy is utilized, to promote the domestic production of conventional energy sources, and to develop new energy sources, particularly renewable sources.

Implementing these programs has been controversial because of varying importance given to different aspects of energy policy. For some, dependence on imports of foreign oil, particularly from the Persian Gulf, is the primary concern; for others, the indiscriminate use of fossil fuels, whatever their origin, is most important. The contribution of burning fossil fuels to global climate change is particularly controversial. Another dichotomy is between those who see government intervention as a positive force and those who view it as a necessary evil at best.

Chapter 4 – The United States has seen a resurgence in petroleum production, mainly driven by technology improvements—hydraulic fracturing and directional drilling—developed for natural gas production from shale formations. Application of both of these technologies enabled natural gas to be economically produced from shale and other unconventional formations, and contributed to the United States becoming the world's largest natural gas producer in 2009. Use of these technologies has also contributed to the rise in U.S. oil production over the last few years. In 2009, annual oil production increased over 2008, the first annual rise since 1991, and has continued to increase each year since then. Between October 2007 and October 2013, U.S.

monthly crude oil production rose by 2.7 million barrels per day, with about 92% of the increase coming from shale and related tight oil formations in Texas and North Dakota. Other tight oil plays are also being developed, and helped raise the prospect of energy independence, particularly for North America.

The rapid expansion of oil and gas extraction using hydraulic fracturing—both in rural and more densely populated areas—has raised concerns about its potential environmental and health impacts. These concerns have focused primarily on potential impacts to groundwater and surface water quality, public and private water supplies, and air quality.

States broadly regulate oil and gas exploration and production on non-federal lands. State laws and regulations governing unconventional oil and natural gas development have been evolving across the states in response to changes in production practices, largely in response to the use of high-volume hydraulic fracturing in combination with directional drilling. However, state regulations vary considerably, leading to calls for more federal regulation of unconventional oil and natural gas extraction activities.

Although several federal environmental laws can apply to certain activities related to oil and gas production, proposals to expand federal regulation in this area have been highly controversial. Some advocates of a larger federal role point to a wide range of differences among state regulatory regimes, and argue that a national framework is needed to ensure a consistent minimum level of protection for surface and groundwater resources, and air quality. Others argue against more federal involvement, and point to the long-established state oil and natural gas regulatory programs, regional differences in geology and water resources, and concern over regulatory redundancy.

The federal role in regulating oil and gas extraction activities—and hydraulic fracturing, in particular—has been the subject of considerable debate and legislative proposals for several years, but legislation has not been enacted. While congressional debate has continued, the Administration has pursued a number of regulatory initiatives related to unconventional oil and gas development under existing statutory authorities.

This report focuses on the growth in U.S. oil and natural gas production driven primarily by tight oil formations and shale gas formations. It also reviews selected federal environmental regulatory and research initiatives related to unconventional oil and gas extraction, including the Bureau of Land Management (BLM) proposed hydraulic fracturing rule and EPA actions.

In: Energy Diversity for Economic Progress ISBN: 978-1-63321-577-1
Editor: Simone Williams

Chapter 1

THE ALL-OF-THE-ABOVE ENERGY STRATEGY AS A PATH TO SUSTAINABLE ECONOMIC GROWTH*

Executive Office of the President

EXECUTIVE SUMMARY

The U.S. energy sector is undergoing a profound transformation. The United States is producing more oil and natural gas, is generating more electricity from renewables such as wind and solar, and is consuming less petroleum while holding electricity consumption constant. These developments have had substantial economic and energy security benefits, and they are helping to reduce carbon emissions in the energy sector and thereby tackle the challenge posed by climate change.

To build on this progress, to foster economic growth, and to protect the planet for future generations, the President has set out an aggressive All-of-the-Above strategy on energy. Some of the recent trends in the energy sector predate the Administration and stem from technological advances and risk-taking by American entrepreneurs and businesses, as well as from government-supported research and other public policies. The All-of-the-Above energy strategy supports these trends through environmentally responsible production of oil and natural gas. In addition, the Administration

* This is an edited, reformatted and augmented version of a report issued May 2014.

has advanced the growth of energy sources with low or zero carbon emissions through programs that support wind, solar, other renewables, and nuclear, and has also helped to reduce energy demand by promoting energy efficiency. The Administration is also supporting an ambitious program of carbon capture, utilization and storage for coal and natural gas power plants and for industrial facilities.

The All-of-the-Above energy strategy has three key elements: to support economic growth and job creation, to enhance energy security, and to deploy low-carbon energy technologies and lay the foundation for a clean energy future. This report lays out these three elements of the All-ofthe-Above energy strategy, and takes stock of the progress that has been made to date and the work that remains to be done.

The recent transformation in the domestic energy sector has been historic.

- **Decades-long trends in energy use are being reversed.** Natural gas consumption has risen 18 percent since 2005. In addition, total energy obtained from wind, solar, and geothermal sources has more than doubled since 2009.
- **Many of these changes are largely unforeseen.** Only eight years ago, baseline projections showed steadily increasing petroleum consumption well into the future. But the Energy Information Administration now projects petroleum consumption to decline starting after 2019. In fact, since its peak in 2007, U.S. gasoline consumption has fallen by 5.5 percent, or half a million barrels per day.

The energy sector has provided key support to the recovery from the Great Recession, and the U.S. economy's exposure to abrupt adverse changes in world oil markets should continue to decline.

- **Rising domestic energy production has made a significant contribution to GDP growth and job creation.** The increases in oil and natural gas production alone contributed more than 0.2 percentage point to real GDP growth in both 2012 and 2013, and employment in these sectors increased by 133,000 between 2010 and 2013. Tens of thousands more jobs have been created in the solar and wind industries. These figures do not account for all the economic spillovers, so the overall impact on the economy of this growth in oil and gas production is even greater.

- **Excluding the crisis-affected year of 2009, the U.S. trade deficit as a percent of GDP is the lowest since the 1990s.** Since its 2006 peak, more than a fifth of the narrowing of the trade deficit as a percent of GDP can be directly attributed to a shrinking trade deficit in petroleum products, as rising domestic production and declining domestic consumption have combined to cut oil imports.
- **The resilience of the economy to international supply shocks—macroeconomic energy security—is enhanced by reducing spending on net petroleum imports and by reducing oil dependence.** The factors that have reduced net oil imports—decreased domestic petroleum demand, increased domestic oil production, more efficient vehicles, and increased use of biofuels—reduce the vulnerability of the U.S. economy to oil price shocks stemming from international supply disruptions. Although international oil supply shocks and oil price volatility will always present risks, empirical evidence presented in this report suggests that further reductions in net petroleum imports will reduce those risks.
- **The United States has emerged as the world's leading producer of petroleum and natural gas.** In 2013, combined production of petroleum, natural gas, and other liquid fuels in the United States exceeded that of Saudi Arabia and Russia. The United States leads in natural gas and is predicted by the International Energy Agency to lead in oil as well within a few years.

The President's All-of-the-Above Energy Strategy will sustain and strengthen this important progress, while deploying low-carbon technologies and laying the foundation for a clean energy future.

- **The United States has reduced its total carbon pollution since 2005 more than any other nation on Earth.** While energy-related CO2 emissions have fallen 10 percent from their peak in 2007, recent projections suggest that emissions could begin to increase again, and more work remains to address this critical imperative. In his 2013 State of the Union address, the President again called on Congress to pass legislation that would provide a market-based mechanism for reducing emissions. Absent a market-based solution, a central goal of national energy policy is to develop and to deploy low-carbon technologies that the market would not otherwise undertake because of the externality of greenhouse gas emissions.

- **The President's All-of-the-Above Energy Strategy embraces natural gas as a transitional fuel, and includes steps to ensure that natural gas development is done responsibly.** Natural gas is comparatively cleaner than many other sources of energy. And while extraction of natural gas raises some environmental concerns, including fugitive methane emissions, the Administration is supporting safe and responsible development including a strategy to address gaps in current data on methane emissions, to reduce "upstream" methane emissions, and—as part of the Quadrennial Energy Review—to identify "downstream" methane reduction opportunities.
- **The All-of-the-Above Energy Strategy supports renewables, nuclear, and other zero-carbon energy sources through research, development, and deployment, and also invests in energy efficiency.** The Interior Department is on track to permit enough renewable energy projects on public lands by 2020 to power more than six million homes; the Defense Department has set a goal to deploy three gigawatts of renewable energy— including solar, wind, biomass, and geothermal—on Army, Navy, and Air Force installations by 2025; as part of the Climate Action Plan, the Federal Government committed to sourcing 20 percent of the energy consumed in Federal buildings from renewable sources by 2020; and the Energy Department supports clean energy technology development and cost reduction across the innovation chain, including through significant loan guarantees and demonstration projects to promote nuclear, renewables, efficiency, and clean coal technologies.

I. Introduction: Elements of the All-of-the-Above Energy Strategy

Over the past ten years, the U.S. economy has undergone a revolution in the production and consumption of energy. Breakthroughs in nonconventional oil and natural gas extraction technology have reversed the decades-long decline in domestic oil and natural gas production. The composition of energy sources has begun to shift: petroleum and coal are now being replaced by natural gas and renewables, cleaner sources with low or zero carbon emissions.

Some of these trends predate the Administration, and the President's All-of-the-Above energy strategy supports these trends and aims to accelerate them in an environmentally responsible way. Other trends are newer, and are driven in part by the President's policies.

The President's All-of-the-Above energy strategy has three key elements: to support economic growth and job creation, to enhance energy security, and to deploy low-carbon technologies and lay the foundation for a clean energy future. This report lays out these three elements of the Allof-the-Above Energy Strategy, and takes stock of the progress that has been made to date and the work that remains to be done.

The energy sector has provided key support to the recovery from the Great Recession. Today, as shown in Figure 1-1, the United States produces more crude oil than it imports. Natural gas production has climbed sharply and natural gas prices have fallen, to the benefit of industry and consumers. Employment in the oil and natural gas extraction sector increased by 133,000 from 2010 to 2013. Many more jobs have been added in sectors that support activity in extractive industries like manufacturing, transportation, construction, restaurants and lodging, as well as local jobs in schools, grocery stores, hospitals, and other establishments in drilling regions. And even more jobs have been induced by the extra spending created by these jobs, given the elevated rate of unemployment during the recovery. The CEA estimates that oil and gas extraction alone contributed 0.2 percentage point to GDP growth in 2012 and 2013—and this large contribution does not include all the economic spillovers. The decline in net petroleum imports has helped to reduce the U.S. trade deficit. And the dramatic growth in renewable electricity generating capacity, especially in wind and solar, has also boosted employment and output during the recovery.

The energy revolution is also making the United States more energy secure. Declining net imports reduce the macroeconomic vulnerability of the United States to foreign oil supply disruptions. In today's deregulated domestic liquid fuels market and globally integrated oil market, an international supply disruption means a jump in prices because of the inelastic short-run demand for oil. But the combination of declining gasoline consumption, increasing domestic crude oil production, increasing fuel economy, and increasing use of biofuels enhances the resilience of the U.S. economy to these oil price shocks. Although international oil supply shocks and oil price volatility will always present risks, empirical evidence presented in this report suggests that reductions in net petroleum imports will reduce those risks. Ultimately, long-term reductions of net oil imports must come from reduced demand and increased use of biofuels, electric vehicles, natural gas, and other substitutes for petroleum in transportation. In addition, the diversification of energy sources through the growth of natural gas and renewables has softened the link between world oil prices and domestic energy prices.

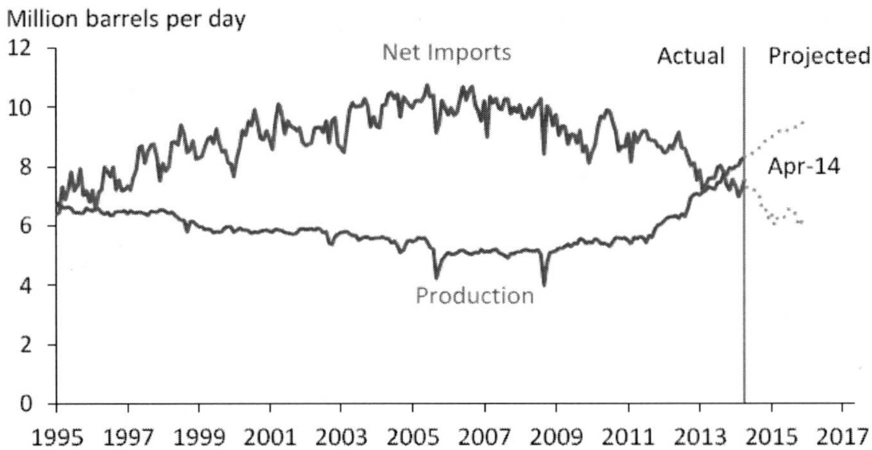

Source: EIA.

Figure 1.1. U.S. Crude Oil Production and Net Imports.

The President's All-of-the-Above energy strategy is also developing and deploying low-carbon technologies and laying the foundation for a clean energy future. From 2005 through 2011 (the last year of data), the United States reduced its total carbon pollution more than any other nation on Earth, in part because of a shift in the United States towards cleaner natural gas and an increasing role for renewables. Although the reductions in CO2 emissions so far are an historic shift from past trends, more work remains, and business-as-usual projections still suggest that CO2 emissions will increase over the rest of this decade as the economy grows. These increasing emissions impose economic and other costs on generations to come—in other words, carbon-intensive energy consumption generates a negative externality that affects the welfare of today's population and their children. Imposing these costs on future generations is irresponsible and our current business-as-usual path is unacceptable.

The President's All-of-the-Above energy strategy makes progress on addressing this critical issue. Natural gas has the lowest CO2 emissions per unit of usable energy produced of any fossil fuel.

Switching from fuels with a greater carbon footprint to natural gas has played a vital role in decarbonizing the energy sector, and will continue to do so for the coming decades. To ensure a small greenhouse gas footprint for natural gas, the Administration is working with States and industry to address the challenges of fugitive emissions of methane (a potent greenhouse gas) and flaring. In addition, through the Department of Energy and the Quadrennial Energy Review, the Administration will identify "downstream" methane reduction opportunities. Renewables will play a central role in a low-carbon energy future. The All-of-the-Above energy strategy supports programs that help to bring down costs of those renewables approaching market readiness, for example through solar programs such as the Department of Energy's SunShot initiative. Absent a comprehensive market-based solution that internalizes the externality posed by carbon emissions, the All-of-the-Above strategy also entails working towards the outcomes of such a solution through policies that include new energy efficiency standards, a continuation of the Renewable Electricity Production Tax Credit, an extended cellulosic fuel tax credit, and direct regulation of carbon emissions.

The Box summarizes some key Administration initiatives under the All-of-the-Above energy strategy.

SELECTED ADMINISTRATION INITIATIVES UNDER THE ALL-OF-THE-ABOVE ENERGY STRATEGY

Electricity

- Issued about $30B in DOE loan guarantees: kickstarted utility-scale solar; supported "first mover" advanced nuclear reactors with enhanced safety features in Georgia; enabled auto industry to retool for very efficient and electric vehicles.
- In partnership with industry, invested in four commercial-scale and 24 industrial-scale clean coal projects that will store more than 15 million metric tons of CO2 per year.
- Under the American Recovery and Reinvestment Act, supported more than 90,000 projects by leveraging nearly $50 billion in private, regional, and state dollars to deploy enough renewable electricity to power 6.5 million homes annually.

- As part of a commitment to improvements in permitting and transmission for renewables, approved 50 utility-scale renewable energy proposals and associated transmission, including 27 solar, 11 wind, and 12 geothermal projects since 2009, enough to power 4.8 million homes. Thirteen of the projects are already in operation.

Transportation

- In 2011, finalized national standards to double the efficiency of light-duty cars and trucks by 2025, reducing oil consumption by 2.2 million barrels a day in 2025 and slashing greenhouse gas emissions by 6 billion metric tons over the lifetime of the vehicles sold during this period.
- Building on the first-ever medium- and heavy-duty vehicle fuel economy standards released in 2011, began collaborating with industry to develop standards for vehicles beyond model year 2018, which will lead to large savings in fuel, lower CO_2 emissions, and health benefits from reduced particulate matter and ozone.

Energy Efficiency

- Since June 2013 alone, issued proposed or final energy conservation standards for eleven products through the Department of Energy. These standards—when taken together with the final rules already issued under this Administration—mean that more than 70 percent of the President's goal of reducing carbon pollution through appliance efficiency standards will be achieved. As a result, by 2030, CO2 emissions will fall by at least 3 billion metric tons cumulatively and save hundreds of billions of dollars in energy costs.
- Launched the Better Buildings Challenge in 2011 to help American commercial and industrial buildings become at least 20 percent more energy efficient by 2020. More than 190 diverse organizations, representing over 3 billion square feet, 600 manufacturing plants and close to $2 billion in energy efficiency financing stepped up to the President's Challenge. This year, 25 new states, cities, school districts, multifamily housing, retailers, food service, hospitality and manufacturing organizations announced they are joining as partners.

- Set an additional $2 billion goal in federal energy efficiency upgrades to Federal buildings over the next 3 years. This challenge, in combination with the initial commitment of $2 billion in 2011, will result in a total of $4 billion in energy efficiency performance contracts in the Federal sector through 2016.
- Beginning in 2009, created weatherization programs that helped low-income households save $250-$500 a year on their energy bills and have provided energy efficiency improvements to nearly 2 million homes.

Oil and Natural Gas

- Worked to reduce processing time for onshore drilling permits, now at the lowest it has been in eight years. In FY 2013, onshore production on Federal and Indian lands increased 37% compared with FY 2008. This year, the Interior Department has already held eight onshore lease sales, generating over $78 million in revenue for States, Tribes, and the American taxpayer.
- Promoted environmentally responsible development of offshore resources through the Interior Department's Five-Year Outer Continental Shelf Oil & Gas Leasing Program. Since the implementation of new safety standards following the Deepwater Horizon incident in 2010, the Interior Department has issued 260 new shallow-water well permits and 229 new deep water well permits.

In addition to policies already undertaken, the President, as part of his FY 2015 Budget, has proposed new initiatives including:

- Investing $5.2 billion in funding for clean energy technology activities at the Department of Energy, including $860 million for programs and infrastructure that support nuclear energy technologies, $700 million to increase affordability and convenience of advanced vehicles and renewable fuels, and $400 million in cleaner energy from fossil fuels.
- Establishing an Energy Security Trust to help fund efforts to shift cars and trucks off of petroleum products, a $2 billion investment over 10 years that will support R&D into a range of cost-effective technologies.

- Putting $839 million towards advancing the goals of the Global Climate Change Initiative (GCCI) and the President's Climate Action Plan by supporting bilateral and multilateral engagement with major and emerging economies.

II. THE ENERGY REVOLUTION AND THE ECONOMIC RECOVERY

The recent changes in the energy sector and their consequences for economic growth have been remarkable. Increasing production of oil, natural gas, and renewable energy has contributed to employment and GDP growth during the recovery, and declining net petroleum imports have helped to reduce the U.S. trade deficit.

The Energy Revolution in Historical Perspective

Over the past two centuries, the amount of energy consumed in the United States has increased dramatically and its mix has changed to sources of energy that are more potent and more convenient. As Figure 2-1 shows, through the middle of the nineteenth century, the main energy source in the U.S. was wood. The use of coal rose sharply through the early twentieth century, then reached a plateau until its use increased in the 1970s for electricity generation. For most of the twentieth century, petroleum consumption grew sharply, dropping off temporarily after the oil crises of the 1970s but then resuming its growth. Natural gas consumption grew during the second half of the twentieth century and has been used increasingly in homes and industry, and to meet peak electricity demand. During the last quarter of the twentieth century, nuclear electricity generation increased to the point that it now supplies 19 percent of electricity, and wood, the original biofuel, saw a small regional resurgence (primarily for home heating) as a result of the increases in home heating oil prices in the 1970s. Meanwhile, renewables production – which includes biomass and biofuels, hydroelectric, wind, solar, and geothermal energy – has surpassed nuclear energy production.

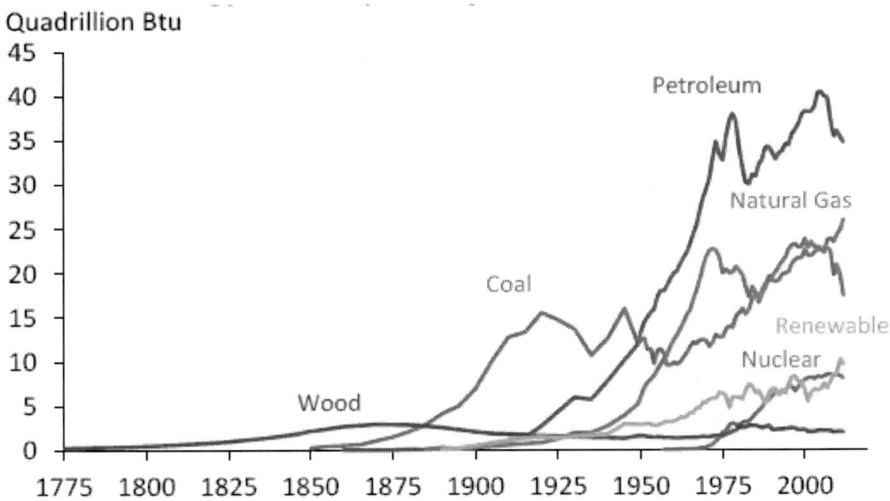

Source: EIA.

Figure 2-1. Energy Consumption by Source, 1775-2012.

These trends have shifted dramatically in the 21st century: the use of coal has declined by 21 percent since its peak in 2005 and total petroleum consumption has declined by 13 percent since its peak in 2005. Because of the revolution in nonconventional natural gas extraction through horizontal drilling and hydraulic fracturing, natural gas consumption has increased sharply, with much of this increase displacing coal for electricity generation. In addition, total energy obtained from wind, solar, and geothermal sources has increased five-fold since 2005.

The decline in petroleum consumption starting in 2006 was unexpected. A standard way to quantify unforeseen developments is to look at revisions to forecasts, because those revisions represent the contribution of new, unforeseen information. In the case of energy, industry-standard benchmark forecasts are produced annually by the Energy Information Administration (EIA) in its Annual Energy Outlook, so revisions to those forecasts quantify the effect of unforeseen developments on the energy sector. Figure 2-2a shows U.S. petroleum consumption since 1950 and forecasted consumption from the 2006, 2010, and 2014 Annual Energy Outlooks. Only eight years ago, these benchmark forecasts projected increasing petroleum consumption over a thirty-year forecast horizon. But events, including the Great Recession—unforeseen at the time of the EIA's 2006 forecasts—unfolded rapidly: by 2010, EIA had reduced both the level and rate of growth of the forecast, and its 2014 outlook now projects petroleum consumption to decline after a slight increase over the next five years. This unforeseen reversal in petroleum demand is led by the reversal in gasoline demand, which is shown in Figure 2-2b: the 2014 EIA projection of consumption in 2030 is 45 percent below the EIA projection made in 2006. The initial decline in the level of consumption is due in part to the recession, but much of the lower projection for the coming decades reflects unforeseen efficiency improvements stemming from the 2012 light-duty vehicle fuel economy standards, along with some projected switching to diesel in the light-duty fleet.

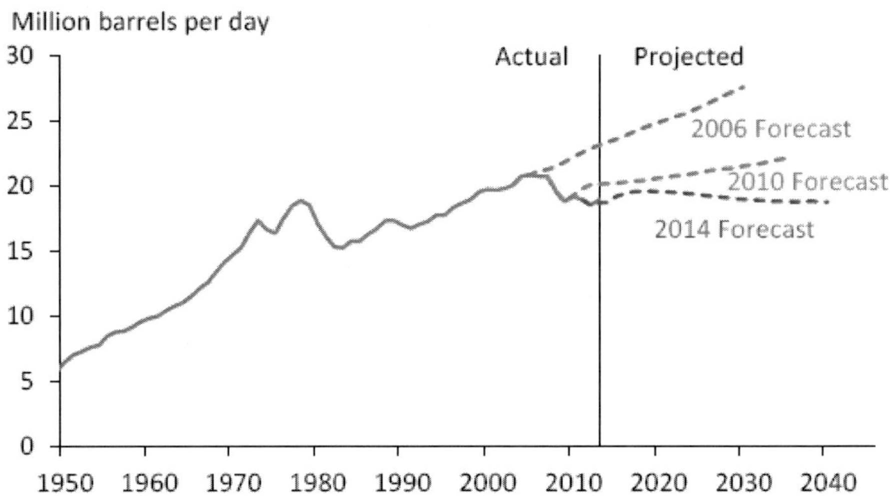

Source: EIA.

Figure 2-2a. U.S. Petroleum Consumption, 1950-2040.

The recent increase in petroleum production was equally unforeseen. As Figure 2-3 shows, domestic petroleum production peaked in 1972 at 11 million barrels per day (bpd). Production plateaued through the mid-1980s and then declined steadily through the late 2000s as conventional domestic deposits were depleted. Since then, however, entrepreneurs adapted horizontal drilling and hydraulic fracturing technology that had been more widely used for natural gas, enabling them to extract oil within the rocky formations of plays once considered exhausted, as in the Eagle Ford in West and South Texas, and to develop new plays as in the Bakken in North Dakota. These developments are both unforeseen and recent: most of the revision to EIA's forecast occurred since 2010, and now EIA projects production to surpass its earlier peak in 2015. EIA projects production to decline slowly after 2019, although because the technology is still advancing there is considerable uncertainty about the economically recoverable resource potential.

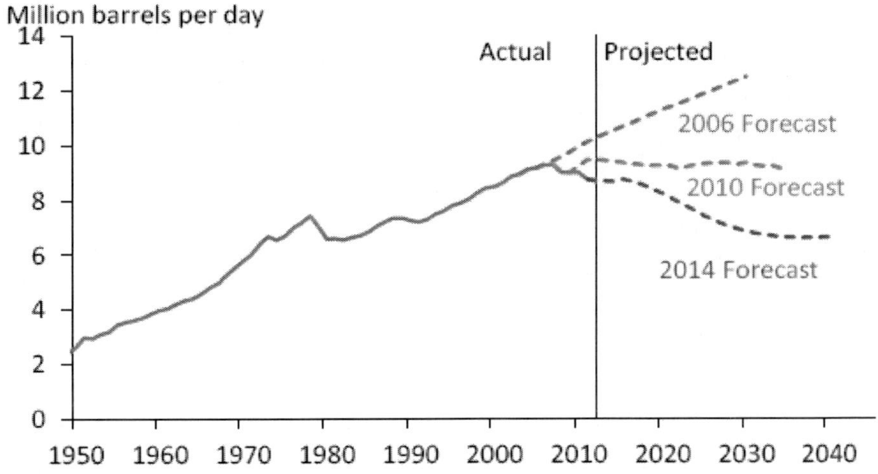

Source: EIA.

Figure 2-2b. U.S. Consumption of Motor Gasoline, 1950-2040.

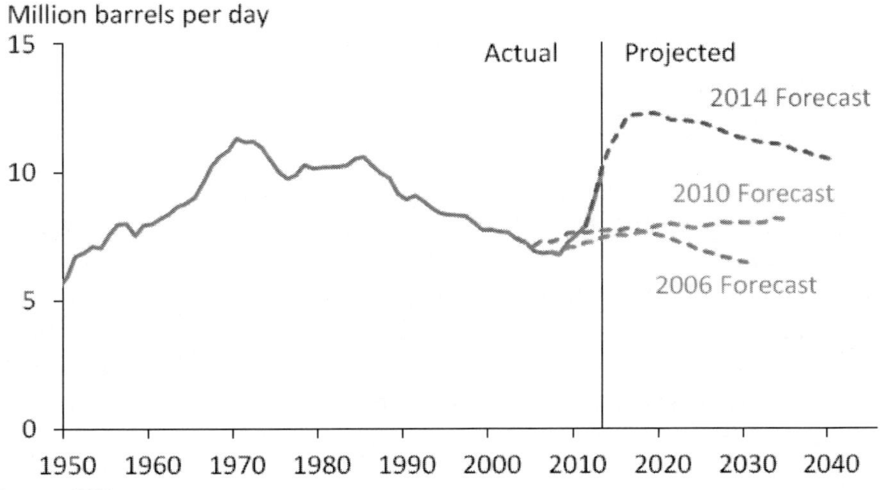

Source: EIA.

Figure 2-3. U.S. Petroleum Production, 1950-2040.

The unforeseen decline in demand for petroleum and increase in oil production has led to a sharp turnaround in net petroleum imports (Figure 2-4), which fell from a peak of over 12 million bpd in 2005 to 6.2 million bpd in 2013—a drop of more than 6 million bpd in 2013, relative to EIA's 2006 forecast of 2013 imports.[1] Of this unforeseen fall in net imports, roughly 4 million bpd, or 65 percent, is due to the unforeseen fall in consumption, and 2 million bpd, or 35 percent, is due to the unforeseen increase in production, relative to the respective 2006 EIA forecasts.

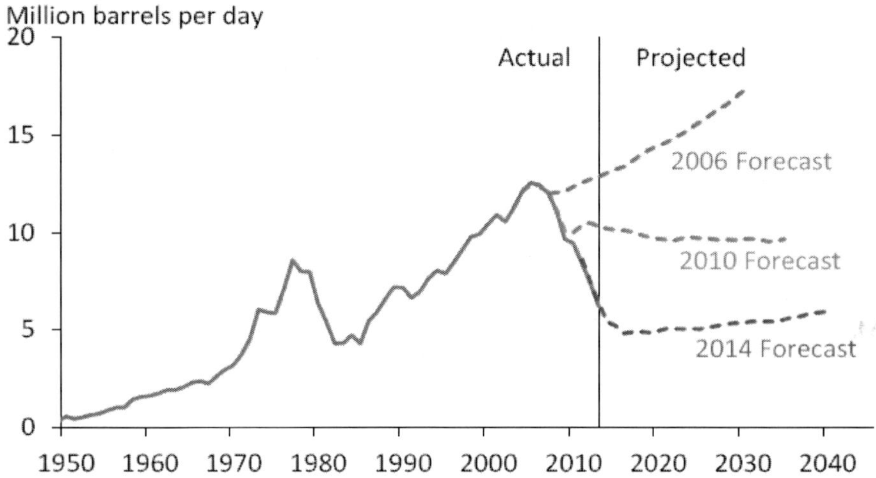

Source: EIA.

Figure 2-4. U.S. Petroleum Net Imports, 1950-2040.

The increase in nonconventional natural gas production preceded the increase in nonconventional oil production. Figure 2-5, which presents domestic natural gas production and historical EIA forecasts, shows that the EIA's 2014 projections indicate increasing natural gas production through 2040. Already, well over half of natural gas production is from nonconventional plays (tight gas and shale gas), a fraction that is projected to increase as the conventional resource base becomes less productive and competitive.

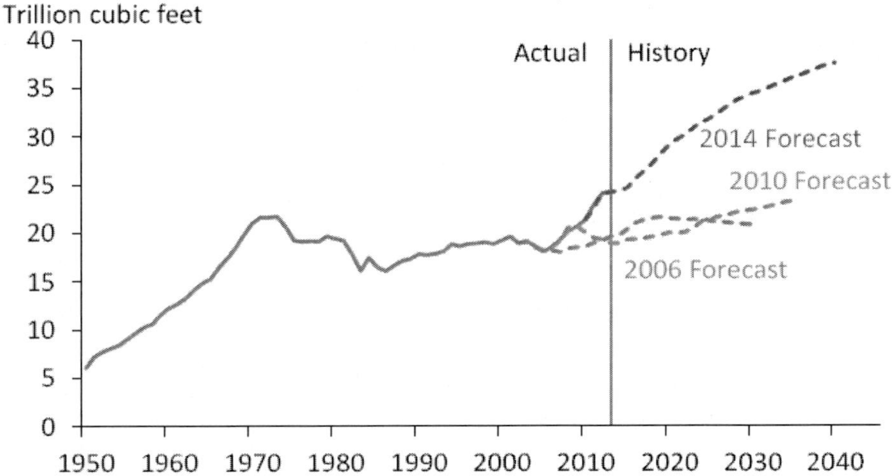

Source: EIA.

Figure 2-5. U.S. Natural Gas Production, 1950-2040.

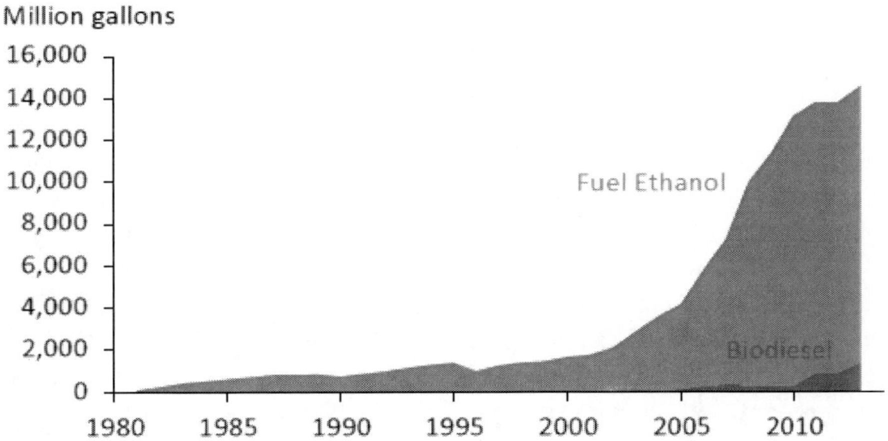

Source: EIA.

Figure 2-6. U.S. Fuel Ethanol and Biodiesel Consumption, 1981-2013 (Annual Rate).

Domestic use of renewable energy sources has also increased substantially since 2000. Figure 2- 6 shows that the use of liquid biofuels—primarily ethanol from corn and biodiesel from various sources including waste oil and soy oil—grew sharply in the mid-2000s as ethanol replaced MTBE as an oxygenate to boost octane and to reduce emissions of aromatic hydrocarbons, further supported by the Renewable Fuel Standard mandates under the Energy Independence and Security Act of 2007. The combined effect of increased production of natural gas, oil, and liquid biofuels has resulted in the United States being the leading petroleum and natural gas producer in the world (Figure 2-7).

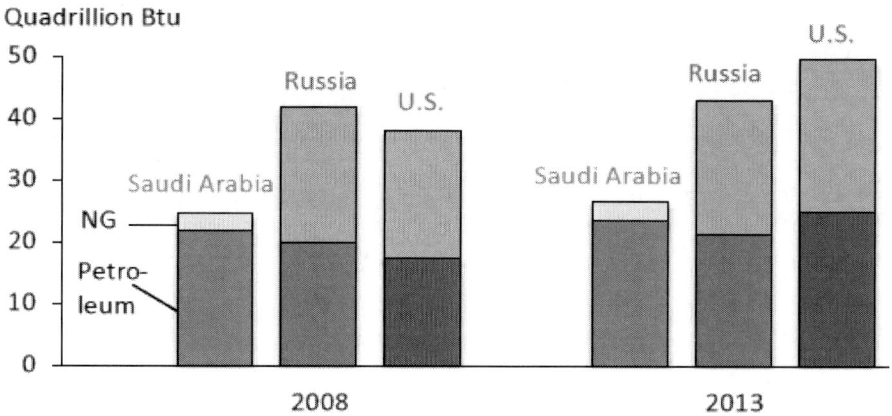

Source: EIA.

Figure 2-7. Petroleum, Natural Gas and Biofuels Production, 2008-2013.

The energy revolution also includes a dramatic increase in the use of renewables. At the end of 2013, wind electricity generation capacity totaled 61 gigawatts, an increase of 140 percent over its 2008 level. In 2012 alone, a record 13 gigawatts of new wind power capacity was installed, roughly double the amount of newly installed capacity in 2011. These 13 gigawatts of new wind capacity represented the largest share of additions by a single fuel source to total U.S. electric generation capacity in 2012. Altogether between 2010 and 2013, total installed wind power generation capacity grew by over 20 gigawatts or 50 percent, with construction throughout the Midwest, Southwest, West Coast, and New England (Figure 2-8). As a result, annual electricity production from wind energy tripled from 2008 to 2013, from 55,363 million kilowatt-hours to 167,567 million kilowatt-hours. Similarly, utility-scale electricity production from solar power grew more than ten-fold from 2008 to 2013, from 864 million kilowatt-hours to 8,918 million kilowatt-hours. Total energy from solar (which in addition to electricity generation includes heating, hot water, and other uses) nearly quadrupled from a monthly rate of 8 trillion Btu to 29 trillion Btu over the same period (Figure 2-9).

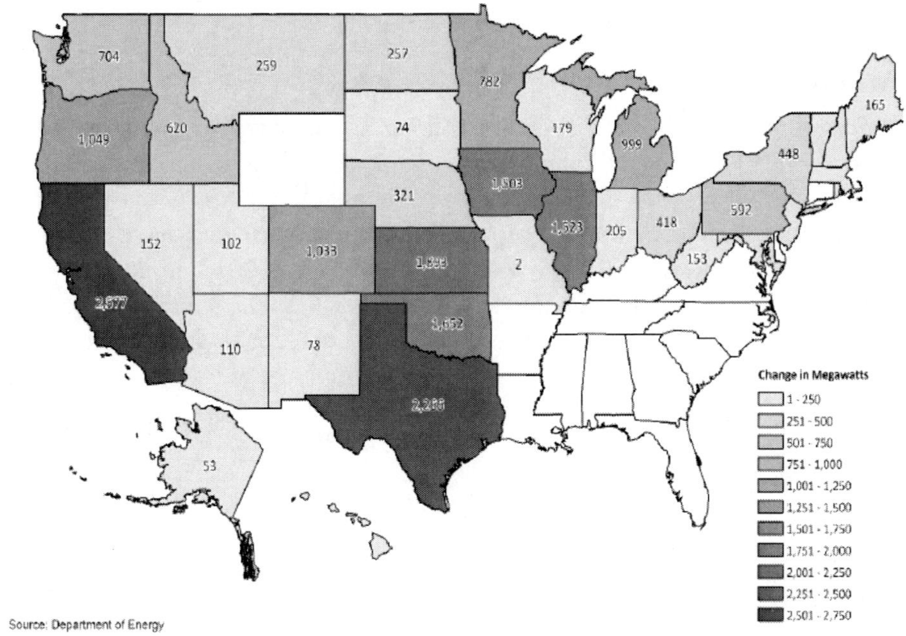

Figure 2-8. Change in Wind Power Generation Capacity, 2010-2013.

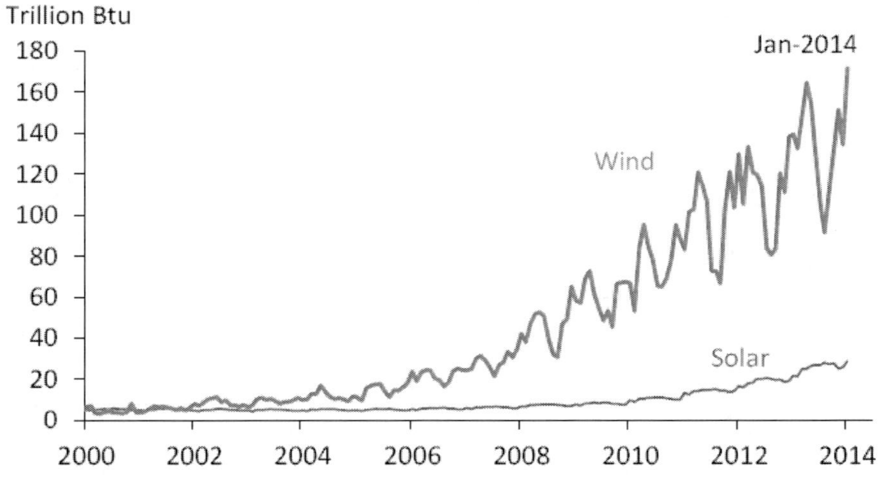

Source: EIA.

Figure 2-9. Total Monthly Wind and Solar Energy Production.

GDP, Jobs, and the Trade Deficit

This U.S. energy revolution has contributed to the growth of the economy—both in terms of economic output as measured by gross domestic product (GDP) and overall employment—and the decline of the trade deficit, as the economy recovered from the Great Recession. CEA estimates that the increase in oil and natural gas production alone contributed more than 0.2 percentage point to real GDP growth in both 2012 and 2013, in contrast to a slight negative contribution on average from 1995 to 2005 (Figure 2-10). This 0.2 percentage point contribution, which does not count all the economic spillovers, added substantially to the 2.3 percent annual rate of growth of the economy as a whole over these two years.

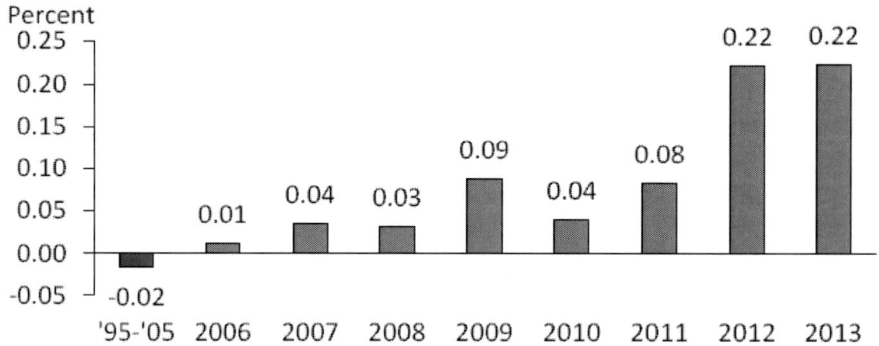

Note: CEA calculations use physical quantity data for oil and natural gas production.
Source: EIA; CEA calculations.

Figure 2-10. Contributions of Oil and Natural Gas Production to GDP Growth.

The growth in oil and gas production has both directly and indirectly created jobs over the past several years. As Figure 2-11 shows, employment in the oil and natural gas extraction sector increased by 133,000 between 2010 and 2013, and continues to grow into 2014. Much of this job growth has been concentrated in a handful of states like Texas, Pennsylvania, Louisiana and North Dakota that are at the forefront of developing their energy resources (see Cruz, Smith and Stanley [2014]). In addition to direct employment in resource extraction, jobs have been created in the companies that provide goods and services to those industries and to their workers, including manufacturing, transportation, and leisure and hospitality. Local jobs in schools, retail, health care, and other sectors have also been created in oil and gas development regions. Because of the elevated unemployment rate during the recovery, the number of indirect jobs, including those created through aggregate demand spillovers, could be quite large: one private estimate holds that nonconventional oil and gas activity contributed a total of 1.7 million jobs in 2012 (IHS CERA [2012]). After falling nearly continuously since the early 1980s, employment in coal mining also edged up slightly over this period and in 2012 stood at approximately 90,000 employees.

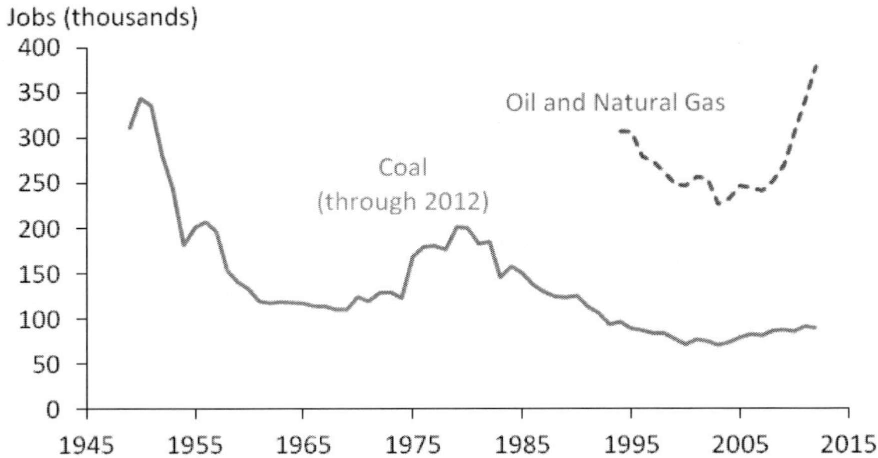

Source: EIA; BLS.

Figure 2-11. Natural Resource Extraction Employment, 1949-2013.

Expansion of renewable energy capacity has also contributed to economic growth. Employment in the renewable sector spans several categories in Federal data collection systems, which complicates direct estimation of employment and output in the sector. However, trade association data suggest that, in addition to rapid expansion in output, there has also been a sharp rise in employment. As Figure 2-12 shows, from 2010 to 2013, employment in the solar energy industry grew by more than 50 percent to almost 143,000 jobs. Moreover, employment in the solar industry is projected to increase by another 20,000 in 2014.[2] Similarly, wind industry employment in 2013 totaled in the tens of thousands.[3]

The increase in domestic oil production, combined with reduced demand for oil, has also led to a sharp drop in net petroleum imports and, as a result, a decline in the trade deficit. In 2006, the total trade deficit was 5.4 percent of GDP, the highest recorded for the United States. By the end of 2013, the trade deficit had fallen to 2.8 percent of GDP, which, excluding the crisis-affected year of 2009, was the lowest since 1999 (Figure 2-13). While the U.S. trade balance is subject to a number of influences and depends in large part on economic conditions in other parts of the world, the rise in domestic energy production has been a substantial factor in the recent improvement. Of the 2.6 percentage point decline in the trade deficit since 2006, about 0.6 percentage point (or just over one fifth) is due to a shrinking trade deficit in petroleum products.

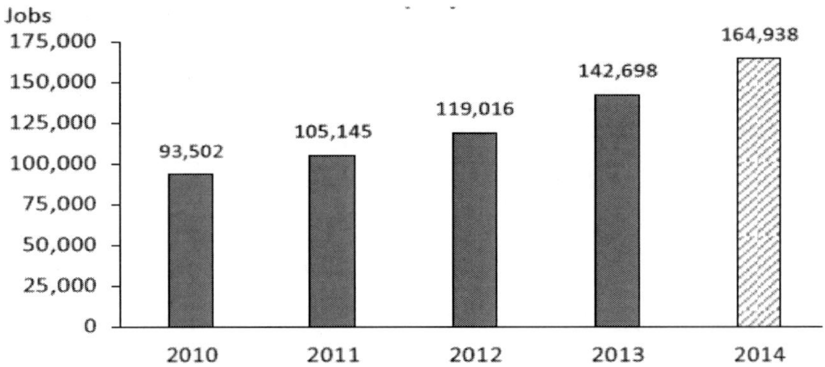

Note: 2014 figure is a projection.
Source: The Solar Foundation.

Figure 2-12. Solar-Related Employment, 2010-2014.

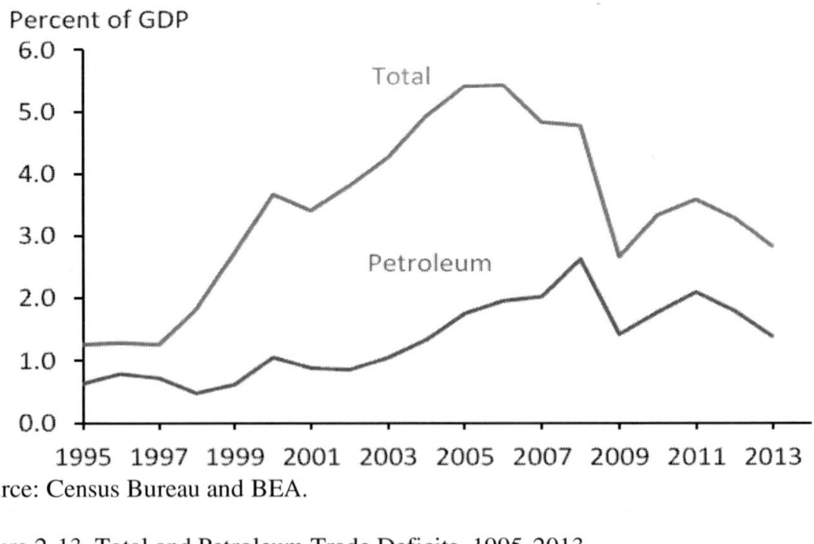

Source: Census Bureau and BEA.

Figure 2-13. Total and Petroleum Trade Deficits, 1995-2013.

Energy Prices, Households, and Manufacturers

Since 2006, natural gas prices have fallen well below crude oil prices on an energy-equivalent basis, providing a cheaper source of energy to consumers and businesses in the United States (Figure 2-14a). Domestic natural gas prices are also well below those in other countries (Figure 2-14b). Today, one million British thermal units (mmBtu) of wholesale natural gas costs around $4.50, roughly half the price paid in Western Europe, a quarter of the price paid in Japan, and a quarter of the price of a comparable amount of crude oil.[4]

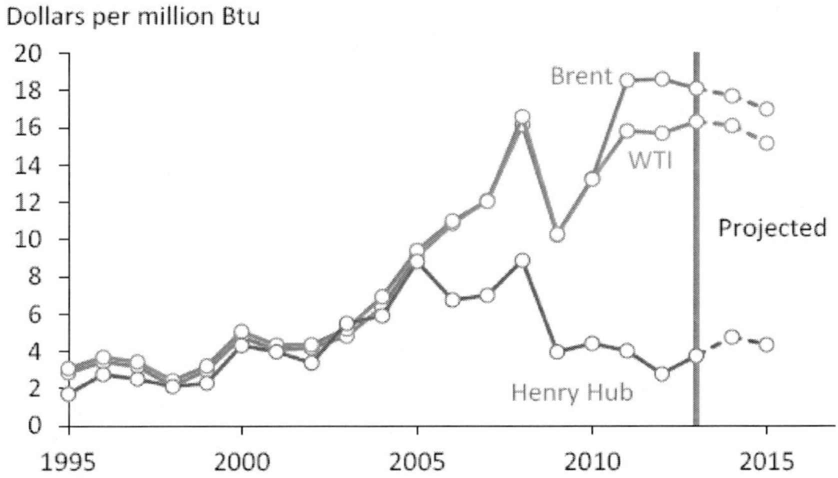

Source: EIA.

Figure 2-14a. Annual Crude Oil and Natural Gas Spot Prices, 1995-2015.

Residential natural gas prices have followed the decline in wholesale natural gas prices, and the twelve-month average price has declined by 20 percent from its 2009 high (Figure 2-15a). Low wholesale natural gas prices have also supported switching fuels in the electric power sector from coal to natural gas. With natural gas prices falling from 2007 to 2012, retail electricity prices have been essentially constant over this period, showing the slowest rate of increase in almost 15 years (Figure 2-15b).

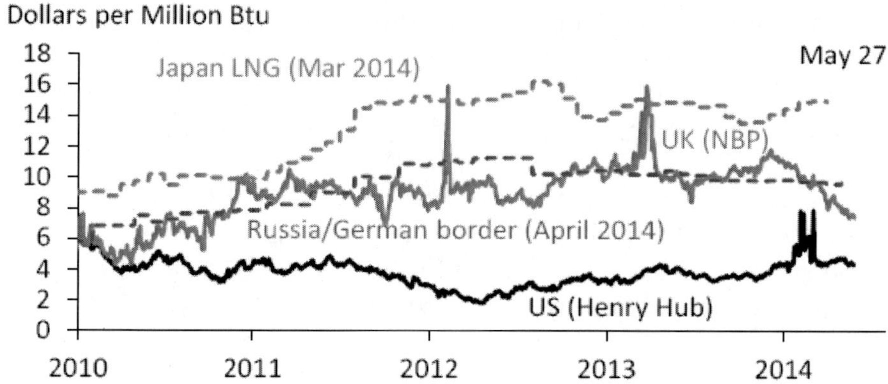

Note: UK's prices do not include natural gas imported from Russia which is predominately indexed to oil prices. Japan and Russia/German border prices are monthly averages.

Source: Bloomberg.

Figure 2-14b. World Natural Gas Spot and Import Prices.

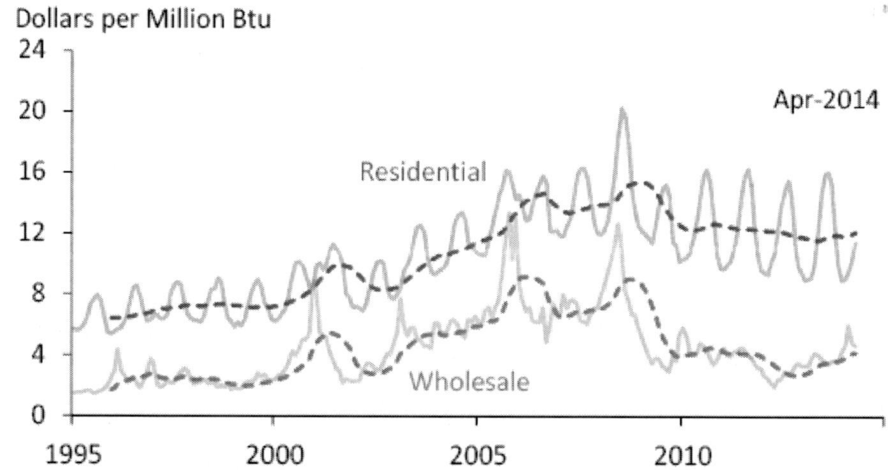

Note: Dashed line represents twelve-month moving average.

Source: EIA.

Figure 2-15a. Wholesale and Residential Natural Gas Prices, 1995-2014.

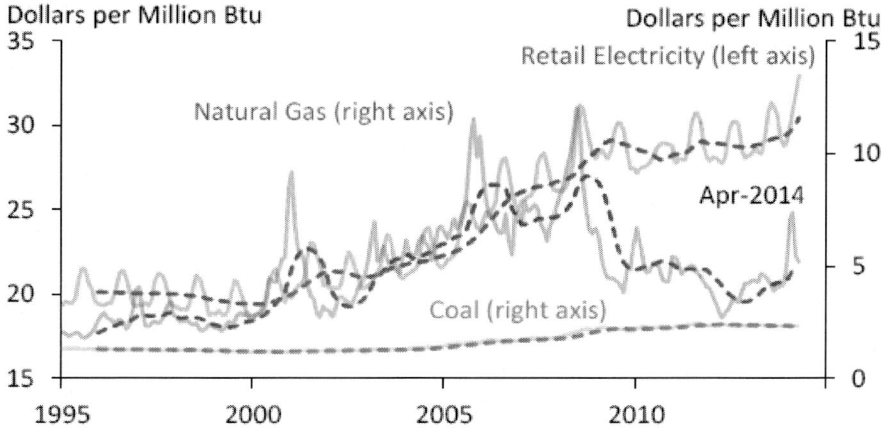

Note: Dashed line represents twelve-month moving average.
Source: EIA.

Figure 2-15b. Retail Electricity Prices and Fuel Costs, 1995-2014.

III. The Energy Revolution and Energy Security: A Macroeconomic Perspective

The term energy security is used to mean different things in different contexts, and broadly covers energy supply availability, reliability, affordability, and geopolitical considerations.[5] This section focuses on macroeconomic energy security, by which we mean the extent to which a country's economic welfare is exposed to energy supply risks, specifically, international energy supply disruptions that lead to product unavailability or price shocks or both. This concept of macroeconomic energy security encompasses domestic risks as well as international supply risks such as disruptions to foreign oil production. In the United States, domestic energy security considerations are important and domestic supply breakdowns can have large costs. For example, the Council of Economic Advisers and the Department of Energy, as well as others, have estimated substantial costs of electricity grid outages associated with storms (CEA/DOE 2013). In its Quadrennial Energy Review, the Department of Energy is broadly examining the U.S. energy infrastructure to identify potential threats, risks, and opportunities for improvement. Historically, however, energy supply disruptions of foreign origin have had the greatest overall macroeconomic impact, notably international oil supply disruptions played a role in the recessions of the 1970s, although disagreement remains about the magnitude of that role. For this reason, this report focuses on the vulnerability of the U.S. economy to international energy supply disruptions.

Table 3-1. Major Oil Disruptions, 1973-2005

Event Name	Date	Duration (months)	Gross Peak Supply Loss (millions of barrels per day)	Percent Change in Oil Prices
Arab Oil Embargo & Arab-Israeli War	Oct-73 to Mar-74	6	4.3	45%
Iranian Revolution	Nov-78 to Apr-79	6	5.6	53%
Iran-Iraq War	Oct-80 to Jan-81	3	4.1	40%
Persian Gulf War	Aug-90 to Jan-91	6	4.3	32%
Civil Unrest in Venezuela	Dec-02 to Mar-03	4	2.6	28%
Iraq War	Mar-03 to Dec-03	10	2.3	28%

Note: Events as identified in Kilian (2008a) and Hamilton (2005). Dates and gross peak supply loss figures as identified in IEA(2012). Price changes for events over select windows as specified in Hamilton (2005) and price changes before 1982 measured using crude petroleum PPI as in Hamilton (2005).

Because 95 percent of U.S. energy import dollars are spent on petroleum, the main threats to U.S. macroeconomic energy security come from international oil supply disruptions. During the OPEC oil embargo of 1973-74, price controls and lack of product led to rationing of gasoline and long queues at service stations. But in today's global oil market with many producers and domestically deregulated petroleum prices in the U.S., petroleum products will still be available in the event of a foreign supply disruption, just at a higher price. Today, macroeconomic energy security concerns the resilience of the U.S. economy to temporary unexpected price hikes—price shocks—of foreign origin.

Historically, temporarily high oil price shocks arising from foreign supply disruptions have cut GDP growth and reduced employment. These events have been studied and debated in depth in the economics literature (starting with Hamilton [1983]; see Hamilton [2009] and Kilian [2008b, 2014] for surveys). Table 3-1 presents a list of the major oil supply disruptions from 1973-2005 identified in Kilian (2008a), the estimated gross peak supply loss, and the percentage change in oil prices in the aftermath of the disruption. For example, in the months following the Iranian Revolution in November 1978, oil prices increased by 53 percent. This link is not perfect, and not every oil price shock has led to an economic slowdown, but as is discussed below in more detail, the empirical evidence points to a negative link between oil price spikes and economic activity.

Trends in Oil Import Prices and Shares

The price of oil plays central roles in macroeconomic energy security. Figure 3-1 shows the price of oil in nominal (current dollars) and in 2013 dollars (deflated by the price index for consumer spending). Jumps in the price of oil are visible around the disruptions of Table 3-1, as well as more gradual increases such as in 2007-08. In real terms, today's oil prices of roughly $100 per barrel are comparable with those in the late 1970s and early 1980s, but are roughly three times the real prices of the 1990s.

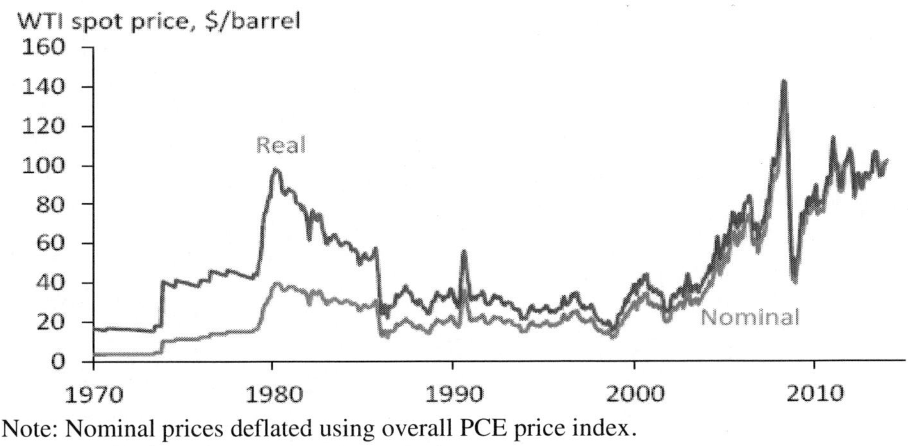

Note: Nominal prices deflated using overall PCE price index.
Source: EIA; Bureau of Economic Analysis.

Figure 3-1. Nominal and Real Oil Prices (2013 $).

The expenditure share of net petroleum imports measures the fraction of GDP that is spent on net imports of petroleum. Ignoring compositional differences, this share is the product of net barrels of petroleum imports times the price per barrel, divided by GDP. Figure 3-2 presents two measures of the expenditure share of GDP of net crude imports. The first uses a narrow definition of net imports of crude, gasoline, distillates, and fuel oil. The second, which is only available since 1973, uses a broader definition that includes other refined products (naphtha, jet fuel, etc.) which slightly increases the share relative to the narrow measure but does not materially change the overall time series pattern. In order to observe longer-term movements, the figure also presents a time series trend of the two measures, which reduces the influence of the high frequency fluctuations in these series that arise from short-term price volatility. For example, during the 1990s the price of oil was low even though physical imports were high, so the expenditure share was relatively low. In contrast, the high oil prices of the past few years have produced a relatively high expenditure share, although this share has declined noticeably over the past few years as domestic demand has declined and domestic oil production has increased.

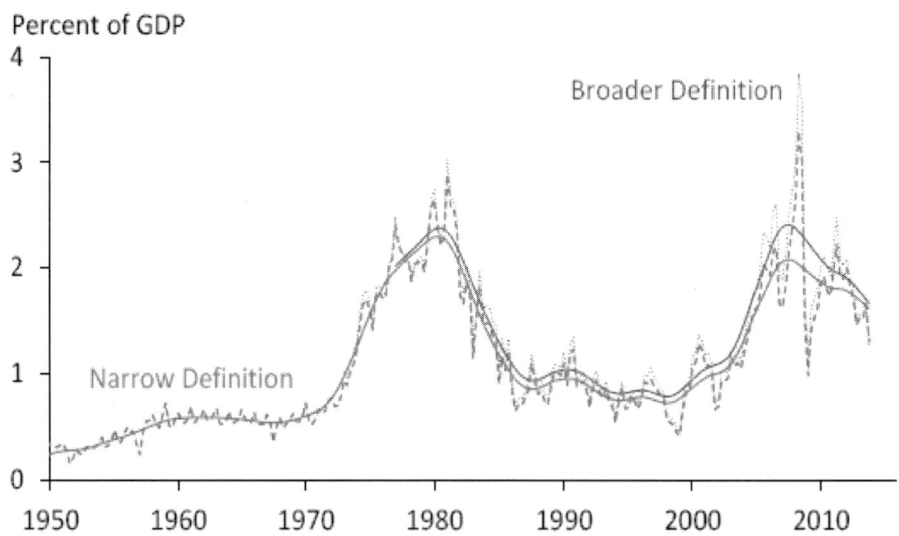

Source: EIA; CEA calculations.

Figure 3-2. Net Import Shares of Petroleum Products.

Macroeconomic Channels of Oil Price Shocks

Oil price shocks can affect the economy through several channels, including consumer demand, the supply of goods and services (production), and physical product rationing. As Kilian (2009) and Blinder (2009) point out, these channels are both conceptually distinct and can have different macroeconomic effects.

Because the demand for petroleum products is inelastic, especially in the short run, the share of expenditures by consumers and firms on petroleum goes up when the oil price increases.[6] Because the Unites States is a net importer of oil, expenditures on net imports increase when the oil price increases. If the oil shock is known to be temporary, the life cycle theory of consumption suggests that consumers would make minimal adjustments to the rest of their spending and would temporarily finance the additional oil consumption through savings. However, in practice consumers do not know the duration of a price hike and many or most would instead reduce their spending on other goods and services to pay for the more expensive fuel needed for daily life. Because expenditures on oil imports go abroad and not to the domestic economy, they do not count towards GDP, so the immediate effect of an increase in the price of an imported good which, like oil, has inelastic demand, is to decrease consumption of domestic goods and services and thus to decrease GDP. This effect on reducing domestic demand is as if the wealth of consumers were reduced, so this channel is sometimes referred to as the wealth channel. This channel can be large. For example, if net oil imports are 2 percent of GDP, as they were in the late 70s and late 2000s, a 10 percent increase in the price of oil causes a reduction in spending on everything else and reduces GDP by 0.2 percent. The extent to which this channel is offset depends on the source of the oil price increase. For example, an increase in overall world economic activity that drives up the demand for and price of oil would expand U.S. exports, at least partially offsetting the increased price of oil imports.

An oil price increase, like a change in the relative price of any other good, also changes the composition of demand as consumers shift spending from items that are indirectly affected by the price increase (like air travel and cars with low fuel efficiency) to goods and services that are less energy-intensive. Thus, products of energy-intensive sectors become relatively more expensive and those sectors will see a reduction in demand, and even within sectors demand can shift across products, such as to cars with greater fuel efficiency. Moreover, to the extent that shifting from energy-intensive goods reduces purchases of durables such as automobiles or refrigerators, spending today is shifted into the future, depressing aggregate demand. Although this compositional shift increases demand in less energy-intensive sectors, it takes time for displaced workers to find alternative employment so incomes decline and unemployment rises (see for example Hamilton [1988]).

An oil price increase can also depress domestic demand if it increases uncertainty. Uncertainty about the economic future can lead consumers to postpone major purchases and can lead firms to postpone investment and hiring, thereby slowing the economy (e.g. Bernanke [1983], Bloom [2009], and for oil investment specifically, Kellogg [2010]). In this channel, oil price volatility can be causal (the volatility creates uncertainty that postpones investment, hiring, or durables consumption), or the volatility can simply reflect broader market uncertainty about future economic or geopolitical events. Another potential demand-side channel is a fall in aggregate consumption because an oil price rise is regressive and transfers income from individuals with a high marginal propensity to consume to individuals with a lower marginal propensity to consume (e.g. Nordhaus [2007]).

Oil price increases can also reduce economic activity through the supply side of the economy. To the extent that energy prices more broadly move with oil prices, an increase in oil prices makes energy a more expensive factor of production, so firms will strive to reduce energy consumption and expenditures. Although capital and labor substitute for energy in the long run, in the short run they can be complements in production because of fixed technologies, so higher energy costs can result in layoffs in energy-intensive firms and industries. Because it takes time for displaced workers to find jobs, incomes decline and unemployment rises. This supply-side channel matters most if price increases are long-lasting, and because capital and labor are being used less efficiently, could also be associated with a slowdown or decline in productivity growth.

The channels discussed so far all concern changes in the relative price of oil and assume that oil is available. If, however, prices are not flexible and instead oil or petroleum products are rationed, the effect on the economy can be severe. On the production side, because energy and labor are complements in the short run, many workers cannot do their jobs without oil. Time spent queuing for gasoline is time not spent productively. In such cases, output falls, and even relatively small dollar volumes of unavailable supply can have an outsized influence on the economy. Fortunately, the development of global crude oil markets and deregulated domestic retail markets have made widespread petroleum product rationing a thing of the past, outside of occasional temporary regional events stemming from weather-related supply chain disruptions. Such events can have significant, even life-threatening impacts on the individuals involved, and minimizing those impacts through improving supply chain resilience is an important goal (and indeed is a central topic of the Department of Energy's Quadrennial Energy Review), but their temporary nature and regional scope means that the macroeconomic impact of the resulting petroleum product unavailability is limited.

Empirical Analysis of Energy Price Shocks

This section presents reduced-form empirical evidence on the relative importance of the different channels of energy supply shocks on the U.S. economy and on the changing correlations among energy prices. The results of this analysis suggest that a lower share of net oil imports in GDP enhances the resilience of the economy to oil price shocks.

The Changing Sensitivity of the U.S. Economy to Oil Price Shocks

The wealth channel makes the concrete prediction that the effect of an oil price shock on GDP growth scales with the share of GDP spent on net oil imports. The scaling of the other channels is less clear without a formal model, but generally those channels would arguably scale either with the importance of oil in the economy (for example, with the consumption expenditure share as examined by Edelstein and Kilian [2009]) or simply affect output directly. For example, the supply-side channels associated with temporary changes in factor prices would depend on elasticities of substitution among factors of production and their shares in production, not shares of net imports, while the uncertainty channel could depend on the overall importance of energy in the economy. If net imports were zero, the wealth effect channel would disappear, but the other channels would still exist.

These observations suggest an empirical strategy in which the effect of the shock is allowed to depend flexibly on the net oil import share, where the degree of dependence is estimated. In addition, the empirical strategy needs to take account of the fact that the effect of an oil shock plays out over a period of many quarters, not all at once. Accordingly, we consider a family of specifications in which an oil price shock has an effect on GDP over several quarters or, equivalently, GDP is affected by current and past values of the oil shock. This suggests the distributed lag model,

$$y_t = c_0 + \sum_{i=0}^{k} c_i \left[\alpha s_{t-i} + (1-\alpha)\mu \right] p_{t-i} + u_t , \tag{1}$$

where y_t is the percentage growth of GDP, p_t is the oil price shock expressed as percent change, *St* is the net oil import expenditure share and *p* is its mean, $C_0,\ldots,C_k$ and *a* are parameters to be estimated, *k* is the number of lags, and *Ut* denotes the other factors determining GDP growth that are not considered in the model. If *a* = 1, then the price shock scales by the share, consistent with the wealth channel, whereas if *a* = 0 then the price shock does not vary over time with the share, consistent with the other channels being more important. Note that in the specification (1), if *a* = 1 and the net import share is zero, oil price shocks have no effect on GDP growth.

To estimate specification (1), we use quarterly data from 1960Q1 – 2006Q4 on real GDP growth, the narrow-concept expenditure share trend in Figure 3-2, and five measures of oil price shocks.[7] Because the oil price increased throughout 2007, peaking in July 2008 just months before the financial crisis, the estimation ends in 2006Q4 so as to avoid overstating oil price effects. The first two oil price shock variables are the quarterly percent change in two oil price measures: the crude petroleum producer price index as used by Hamilton (1996, 2003, 2009) (quarterly average of monthly data) and the spot price of West Texas Intermediate crude ("WTI", collected by the Energy Information Administration; quarterly average of monthly data). Although movements in oil prices are sometimes conveniently treated as exogenous, oil prices respond to economic conditions and there is a large, thoughtful literature that tackles the problems posed by this potential endogeneity (see for example Bernanke, Gertler, and Watson [1997], Barsky and Kilian [2002], Hamilton [2009], Kilian [2008b, 2009], and Ramey and Vine [2010]). The next two measures therefore aim to isolate exogenous movements in oil prices, thereby to reduce the chance of *pt* being correlated with the other shock that comprise *Ut* in specification (1): Hamilton's (1996) net oil price increase variable, which is the percent by which the crude oil producer price index surpasses its previous 12-quarter peak, and zero if it does not (aggregated to the quarterly level as in Hamilton [2009]), and Ramey and Vine's (2010) oil shock variable, which is the residual from a regression of time-adjusted gasoline prices on four current and past macroeconomic variables and thereby aims to capture the exogenous gasoline expenditure shock associated with a potentially endogenous oil price hike (monthly shocks aggregated to quarterly; available 1964- 2013).

The final shock variable measures *ex-ante* volatility of oil prices, not the level, and thus pertains to the supply-side and uncertainty channels; specifically, this series measures volatility as estimated using a GARCH(1,1) model of the percentage change of the monthly WTI spot price (estimated on monthly data 1947-2013, aggregated to quarterly by averaging).[8] This measure, plotted in Figure 3-3, shows considerable variation, with the greatest percentage volatility occurring in the 1970s and before and during the 2007 recession, and relative quiescence during the mid- and late-1990s.

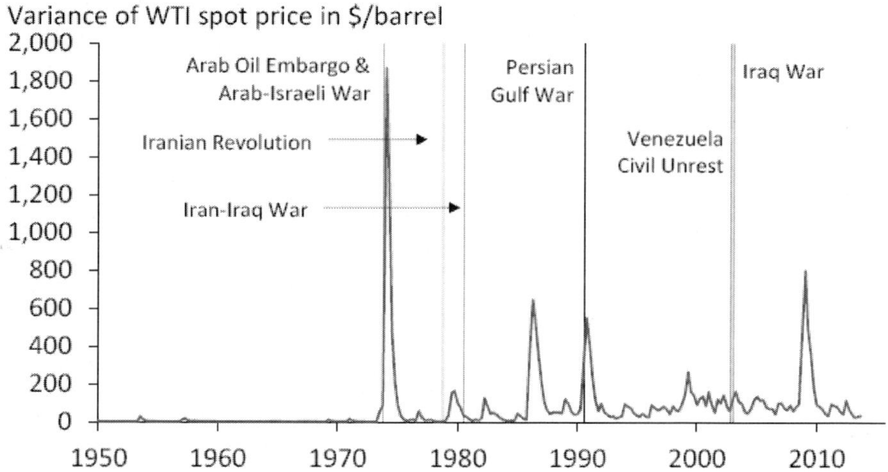

Source: EIA; CEA calculations.

Figure 3-3. Estimated Ex-Ante Volatility of Oil Prices.

The results of estimation of the distributed lag specification (1) for GDP growth and consumption growth using eight lags are summarized in Table 3-2. The table presents estimated values of α, a test of the joint significance of the distributed lag coefficients, and a test of the significance of the 6-quarter cumulative effect; the coefficients themselves are not reported to save space. For GDP growth, for all oil variables except for the Hamilton net oil price increase, the estimated value of α is one, so that for the oil variables and the Ramey-Vine shock the effect of an oil price shock on GDP is proportional to the net import share, which varies over time. In all cases, the estimated effects are negative as expected, typically increasing in magnitude over the first 3-6 quarters. In addition, the dynamic effects are jointly statistically significant and the cumulative 6- quarter effect is individually statistically significant for all dependent variables. The results are similar for consumption growth.

Table 3-2. Empirical Results

Dependent Variable: Real GDP					
Price Shock Variable	WTI (%change)	PPI-Crude (%change)	Hamilton (1996) Price Shock	Ramey-Vine Shock	WTI Volatility
Shock Scale Parameter, α	1	1	0.224	1	1
Standard Error	--	--	0.346	--	--
P-value of F-test of all lag coefficients	<0.0001	<0.0001	<0.0001	<0.0001	<0.0001
T-test of 6-quarter Cumulative Effect	-2.14	-2.62	-3.17	-1.87	-2.45
P-value	0.034	0.009	0.002	0.063	0.015
Dependent Variable: Real PCE					
Price Shock Variable	WTI (%change)	PPI-Crude (%change)	Hamilton (1996) Price Shock	Ramey-Vine Shock	WTI Volatility
Shock Scale Parameter, α	1	1	0.342	1	1
Standard Error	--	--	0.332	--	--
P-value of F-test of all lag coefficients	<0.0001	<0.0001	<0.0001	<0.0001	<0.0001
T-test of 6-quarter Cumulative Effect	-3.34	-3.61	-3.91	-1.25	-2.30
P-value	0.001	<0.0001	<0.0001	0.212	0.022

Note: Entries are results from estimation of the distributed lag model in Equation (1) by by nonlinear least squares, where αwas parameterized using a logistic transformation to impose $0 \leq \alpha \leq 1$. Standard errors in the distributed lag specifications are autocorrelation robust. Standard errors for αare given only for interior estimates because of changes in sampling distributions at the boundary.

In economic terms, the variation over time of the effect of an oil shock on GDP growth implied by the estimated share specifications is substantial. Figure 3-4 shows the estimated dynamic effect on real GDP of a ten percent increase in the WTI spot price, estimated over the full data set (this is the so-called impulse response function associated with the estimated specification for WTI summarized in Table 3-2). For example, when the expenditure share is 2.2 percent, approximately its value at its peaks in 1980 and 2007, the time-series estimates imply that a ten percent increase in the price of oil is associated with a 0.5 percent fall in GDP after 6 quarters. In contrast, when the expenditure share is 0.9 percent, approximately its value in the mid-1990s, this effect on GDP is roughly -0.2 percent. Because the net petroleum import share was substantially lower in second half of 1980s through 1990s than in the late 1970s and early 1980s, these findings are consistent with the reduced effect of oil shocks on GDP found from the mid-1980s through the end of the century (for example, Hooker [1996], Nordhaus [2007], Blanchard-Galí [2010]).

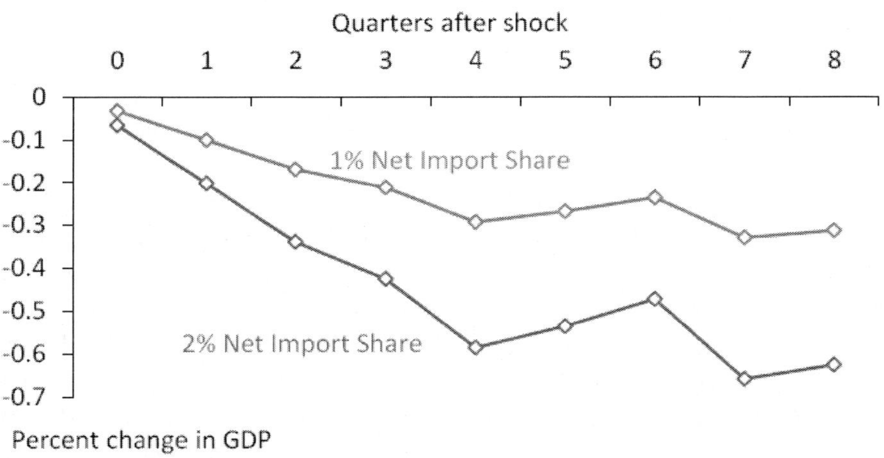

Source: EIA; CEA calculations.

Figure 3-4. Estimated Cumulative Effect a 10% Oil Price Shock on GDP.

Taking these estimates at face value for the moment, they are somewhat larger than would be suggested by the wealth channel alone: for a net oil import share of 2.2 percent, the direct wealth effect of a 10 percent increase in oil prices would be to reduce GDP by 0.22 percent. Even with a Keynesian demand multiplier of 1.5, the reduction would be only 0.33 percent, or roughly two-thirds of the estimated 0.5 percent reduction. Although the estimated 0.5 percent reduction is within a 95% confidence interval of 0.33, these estimates are consistent with meaningful contributions by channels beyond the wealth effect.

The net expenditure share is currently relatively high in historical terms, at 1.8 percent, but is declining sharply. Because of declining demand for transportation fuel and increasing domestic production, the net expenditure share is projected to fall to the historically low level of 1 percent by 2017 under the AEO 2014 reference case. For the oil price specifications reported in Table 3- 2, this projected decline in the net oil import share corresponds to large reductions of the sensitivity of the U.S. economy to oil price shocks.

These results are robust to changes in the estimation sample and to alternative econometric specifications, and aside from the Hamilton net oil price increase are robust to alternative shock measures.[9] Still, they are subject to a number of caveats. Most importantly, oil price changes can occur for multiple reasons, including response to increasing demand; that is, oil price changes are in general not exogenous, so the impulse response functions displayed in Figure 3-4 (or those obtained using the other oil price variables in Table 3-2) should be viewed as describing dynamic correlations and not as causal effects. Identifying causal effects of oil price shocks is a central challenge of this literature, and doing so requires a credible strategy to isolate exogenous variation in the shocks. Identification approaches include formulating multivariate models which embed identifying assumptions (e.g. Bernanke, Gertler, and Watson [1997], Blanchard and Galí [2010], Kilian [2009], Baumeister and Peersman [2013], Kilian and Murphy [2014]) or using an instrumental variables approach (Hamilton [2003], Stock and Watson [2012]). The task of merging the variable-share specification with those approaches to identification is left to further work. Additionally, while the findings here point towards declining oil import shares as being an important reason for the reduced macroeconomic effect of oil price shocks, they do not rule out other factors, such as a changing mix of supply and demand shocks (e.g. Kilian [2009]), as contributing to this reduction. Finally, although the oil shock enters the specifications here nonlinearly in that it is interacted with a function of the share, this analysis does not examine whether these results resolve the findings in the literature on nonlinear oil price effects (see Hamilton [2010], Kilian and Vigfusson [2014], and Kilian [2014] for a review). For all these reasons, the results in Table 3.2 should be viewed as suggestive.

Energy Supply Diversification and Falling Correlations among U.S. Energy Prices

This empirical work so far has focused on the role of oil in macroeconomic energy security. Another aspect of macroeconomic energy security is the extent to which oil price changes produce broader movements in energy prices. Preliminary empirical evidence suggests that, for the United States, the boom in natural gas production has contributed to an attenuation of the link between oil price changes and other energy price changes.

As discussed above, the boom in nonconventional gas production detached the Henry Hub wholesale natural gas price from oil prices (Figure 2-15a). This detachment of the levels of the prices is also reflected in a reduced correlation of price changes. For the five years from 2001- 2005, the correlation between monthly percent changes in the Henry Hub price and the WTI spot price was 0.43. From 2006-2010, this correlation fell to 0.19, and for the four years from 2010 to the present it is -0.17. Consistent with the declining correlation between oil and natural gas prices, the correlation between oil prices and wholesale electricity prices fell from 0.16 during 2000-2005 and 0.27 during 2006-2010 to -0.10 during 2010 to the present.

Discussion

Oil price shocks affect the economy through many channels. In addition to the wealth effect, those channels include shifts in the composition of domestic consumption, adjustments by firms facing a shift in the relative costs of their inputs, and reduced demand from heightened uncertainty. As Edelstein and Kilian (2009) emphasize, oil price shocks depress consumer sentiment. And, because gasoline is needed for routine transportation, oil price shocks are regressive.

Nevertheless, these results support the view that U.S. macroeconomic energy security is enhanced by reducing net petroleum imports, and they underscore the importance of reducing the dependence of the U.S. economy on petroleum. Recently, the net import share has been declining for a combination of reasons: declining demand for transportation fuels, increased domestic oil production combined with increasing refined product exports, and increasing use of biofuels. Thus further contributions to macroeconomic energy security can come from further improvements in fuel economy, as supported by the light- and heavy-vehicle standards; from reducing petroleum demand by shifting to natural gas and electricity as transportation energy sources; from supporting additional, environmentally responsible domestic oil production; and from further use of advanced, low-greenhouse gas biofuels.

IV. A PATH TO A LOW-CARBON FUTURE

A central challenge of energy and environmental policy is to find a responsible path that balances the economic benefits of low-cost energy, the social and environmental costs associated with energy production, and our duty to future generations. As part of the United Nations Climate Change Conferences in Copenhagen and Cancún, the United States pledged to cut its carbon dioxide (CO2) and other greenhouse gas emissions in the range of 17 percent below 2005 levels by 2020. Approximately 87 percent of U.S. anthropogenic emissions of all greenhouse gases (primarily CO2 and methane) are energy-related, and fossil-fuel combustion accounts for approximately 94 percent of U.S. CO2 emissions (EPA 2010).

From an economist's perspective, greenhouse gas emissions impose costs on others who are not involved in the transaction that creates the emissions; that is, greenhouse gas emissions generate a negative externality, of which much is borne by future generations. Appropriate policies to address this negative externality would internalize the externality, so that the price of emissions reflects their true cost, or would seek technological solutions that would similarly reduce the externality. Such policies incentivize energy efficiency and clean energy production.

In his 2013 State of the Union address, the President called on Congress to pass legislation that would provide a market-based mechanism for reducing emissions. Congress has failed to act but the Administration has other tools with which to deploy low-carbon technologies, including tax incentives for investment in and production of clean energy, and direct regulation of greenhouse gas (GHG) emissions, such as the 2012 light-duty fuel economy standards and the regulation of CO2 emissions by fossil fuel fired electric generators under the Clean Air Act.[10]

The United States has made important progress in reducing GHG emissions. As Figure 4-1 shows, energy-related CO2 emissions have fallen 10 percent from their peak in 2007. Given a counterfactual, or baseline, path for these variables, one can attribute the change in carbon emissions to a change in the carbon content of energy, a change in the rate of improvement of energy efficiency, and a change in the level of GDP, relative to the baseline path.[11]

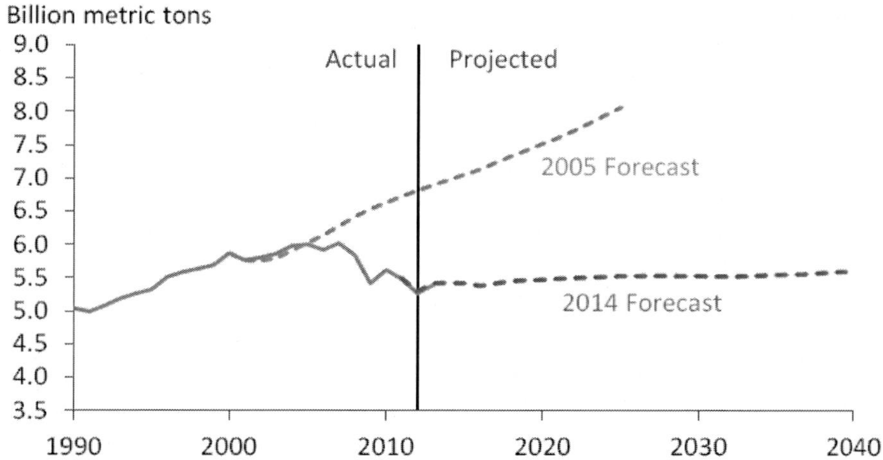

Source: EIA.

Figure 4-1. Energy-Related Carbon Dioxide Emissions.

The baseline path is computed using a combination of historical trends and published forecasts as of 2005. Relative to this baseline, slightly more than half of the decline is due to slower growth than projected in 2005, that is, because of the decline in economic activity as a result of the Great Recession. Slightly less than half the reduction is due to cleaner energy, primarily the reduction in electricity generated by coal and the increase in cleaner natural gas and zero-emissions wind and solar generation. Improvements in energy efficiency made a small contribution: although economy-wide efficiency improved over this period, it improved only slightly faster than the rate projected by the Energy Information Administration in 2005. This analysis of the recent reduction in emissions shows that while progress has been made, much more remains to be done.

The All-of-the-Above energy strategy develops and deploys low-carbon technologies and lays the foundation for a clean energy future. This support ranges from research and experimentation funding for new energy technologies to supporting large-scale deployment. The transition to a low-carbon future is also supported through direct regulation of carbon emissions under the authority of the Clean Air Act, and the Environmental Protection Agency is developing regulations to reduce CO2 emissions from fossil fuel electric generating units as part of the President's Climate Action Plan.

Reducing Emissions through Improved Efficiency

The amount of energy used to produce a dollar of real GDP has declined steadily over the past four decades, and today stands at less than half of what it was in 1970 (Figure 4-2). This improvement in overall energy efficiency, which has averaged 1.5 percent per year since 1960, is due in part to more efficient use of energy resources to complete the same or similar tasks, and in part to shifts in the types of tasks undertaken. Figure 4-2 also presents the Economy-Wide Energy Intensity Index developed by the Department of Energy, which estimates the amount of energy needed to produce a basket of goods in one year, relative to the previous year. Between 1985 and 2011, the DOE Energy Intensity Index fell by 14 percent. In contrast, the energy-GDP ratio fell by 36 percent. Thus, while much of the decline in energy usage per dollar of GDP has come from improvements in energy efficiency, much of it has also come from other factors such as shifts in the composition of output, in particular shifts from more to less energy-intensive sectors of the economy.

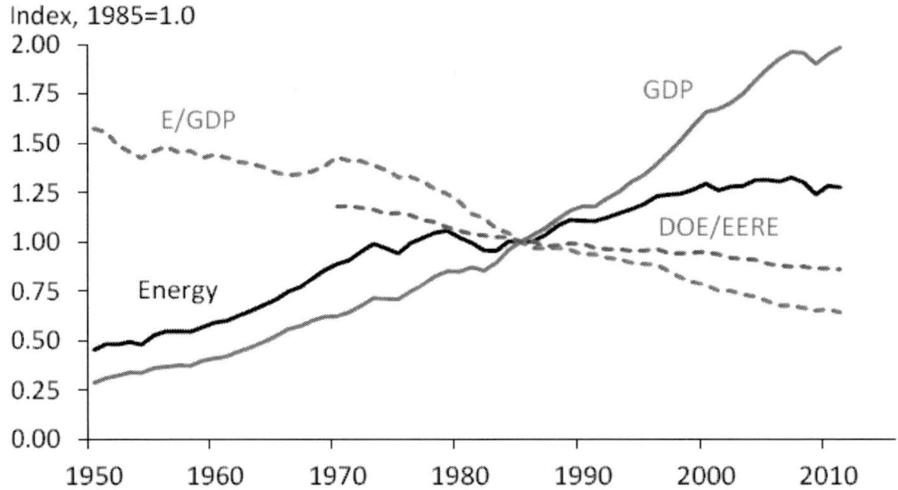

Source: EIA.

Figure 4-2. U.S. Energy Intensity, 1950-2011.

Both market forces and government programs spur energy efficiency improvements. For example, as Figure 4-3a shows, gasoline demand per capita rose through the early 2000s and plateaued in the mid-2000s before dropping substantially during the recession. As the economy recovered, however, gasoline demand per capita continued to fall.

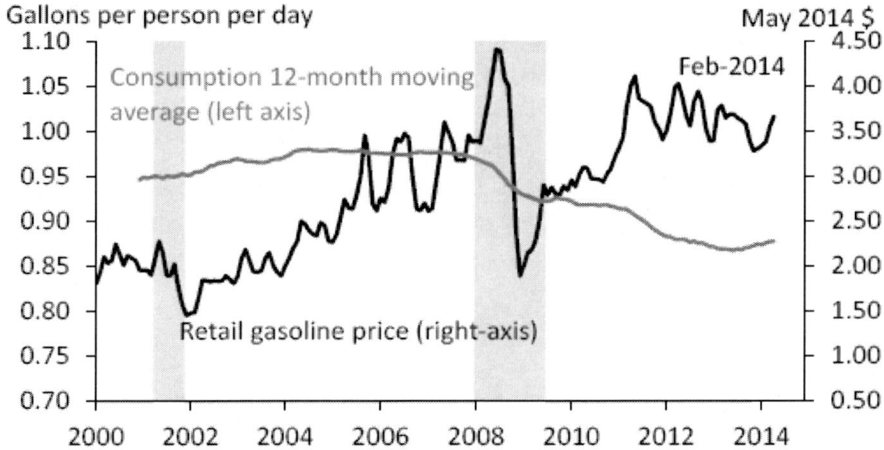

Source: EIA; Census Bureau; CEA calculations.

Figure 4-3a. U.S. Per Capita Gasoline Consumption.

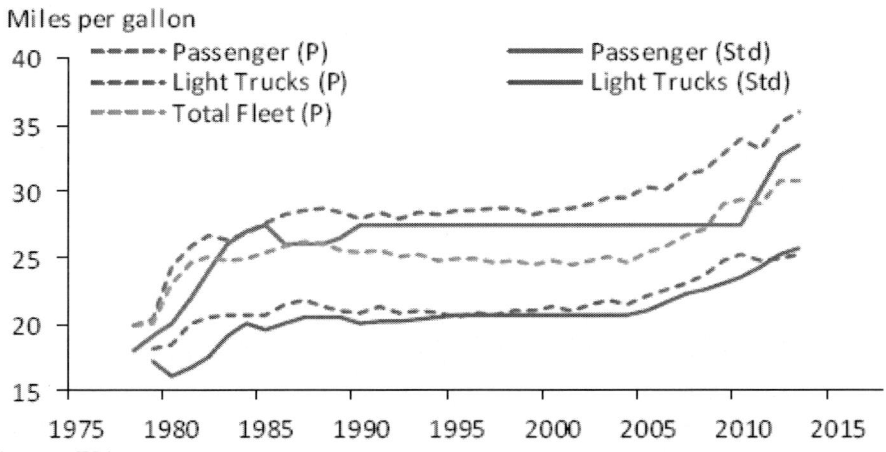

Source: EIA.

Figure 4-3b. Corporate Average Fuel Economy Standard and Performance, 1978-2013.

Some of this continued decline in gasoline demand stems from the relatively high real gasoline prices shown in Figure 4- 3a, but that is only a partial explanation. Increasing fuel efficiency brought about by Federal fuel economy standards also played a role. In 2012, the Administration finalized fuel economy standards that, together with the Administration's first round of standards, will nearly double from 2010 levels the fuel economy of light duty vehicles to the equivalent of 54.5 miles per gallon by the 2025 model year (Figure 4-3b). Furthermore, beginning in model year 2014, medium- and heavy-duty trucks must meet new energy efficiency standards as well, which are projected to increase their fuel efficiency by 10 to 20 percent by 2018.

As mentioned earlier in this report, the Administration has also undertaken a number of other initiatives as part of its All-of-the-Above Energy Strategy to boost energy efficiency in buildings, appliances, and its own operations.

Natural Gas as a Transitional Fuel

Natural gas is already playing a central role in the transition to a clean energy future. According to the decomposition mentioned above, nearly half of the CO_2 emissions reductions from 2005 to 2013 came from fuel switching, primarily switching from the use of coal to natural gas, wind, and solar for the purpose of generating electricity. Nonconventional natural gas development has opened a vast resource, and, as shown in Figure 4-4, the Energy Information Administration projects increasing quantities of natural gas production along with low prices over the coming two decades.

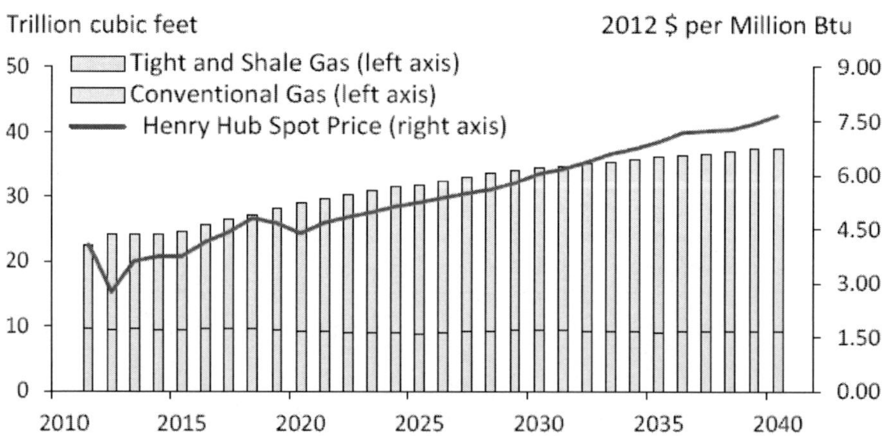

Source: EIA.

Figure 4-4. U.S. Natural Gas Production and Wholesale Prices, 2011-2040.

A leading reason for the increased use of natural gas for electricity production is that its price fell. As Figure 4-5 shows, the decline in natural gas prices in 2008-9 and in 2012 induced substitution of natural gas for coal in electricity generation. In 2013, the benchmark natural gas price increased from \$3.33 per mmBtu in January 2013 to \$4.24 per mmBtu in December 2013, and as natural gas prices rose relative to coal, the use of coal for electricity generation increased while the use of natural gas decreased. Looking ahead, the relatively low price of natural gas will make it an economically attractive alternative fuel as regulation of CO2 and other emissions under the Clean Air Act further reduces coal-fired electricity generation.

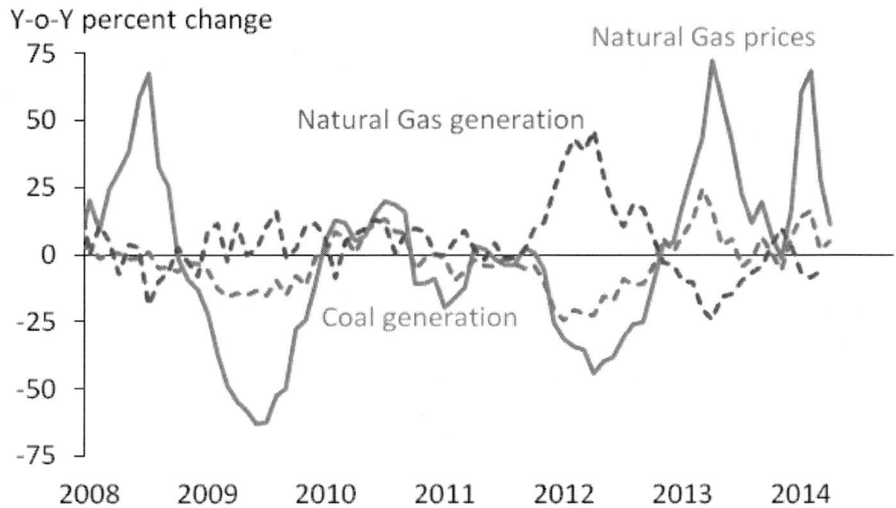

Source: EIA.

Figure 4-5. Change in Monthly Electricity Generation and Prices.

It is important that this expansion of natural gas production be done responsibly and with environmental safeguards. Environmental concerns associated with natural gas include fugitive methane emissions (methane is a potent greenhouse gas), flaring, and local environmental issues associated with water and land use for hydraulic fracturing operations. As part of the Climate Action Plan, the Administration is undertaking a strategy both to reduce methane emissions and to address gaps in current data on methane emissions. The regulatory structure for addressing local environmental concerns, especially around land and water use, exists primarily at the state and local level. Research that will inform prudent local environmental regulation of hydraulic fracturing is actively under way.

Looking further ahead, developing natural gas generation infrastructure now prepares for future widespread deployment of wind and solar generation.

Wind and solar are non-dispatchable because of variable wind speeds and insolation, so both need either storage or backup generation capacity. Developing base load natural gas infrastructure today facilitates its use tomorrow for peak demand and renewable backup generation.

Supporting Renewables, Nuclear, and Clean Coal

Low- and zero-carbon renewable, nuclear, and clean coal energy sources have a central role to play in a clean energy future. Consequently, the President's All-of-the-Above strategy makes a strong commitment to supporting these technologies.

Electricity from Wind and Solar Energy

Wind and solar generation are zero-emission sources of energy and thus do not create a negative climate externality. If emissions were priced to internalize the climate externality, then, wind, solar, and other renewable energy sources would therefore enjoy an additional price advantage beyond current market prices. In the absence of market-based mechanisms to internalize the externality, it is appropriate to provide support through tax incentives and other measures commensurate with the value of the GHG reductions provided by those zero-emissions energy sources. Accordingly, the Administration backs such support for renewables, including the renewable energy production tax credit. In addition, the Administration supports early deployment projects aimed at bringing down the ultimate market price of renewables.

Government support, increasing competitiveness of wind and photovoltaic electricity production, and renewable portfolio standards that many states have adopted have together increased the share of electricity generated by non-hydro renewables from roughly 2 percent in 2007 to 6 percent in 2013 (Figure 4-6). Since the beginning of 2011, the average cost of solar panels has dropped more than 60 percent and since the beginning of 2010 the cost of a solar photovoltaic electric system has dropped by about 50 percent.

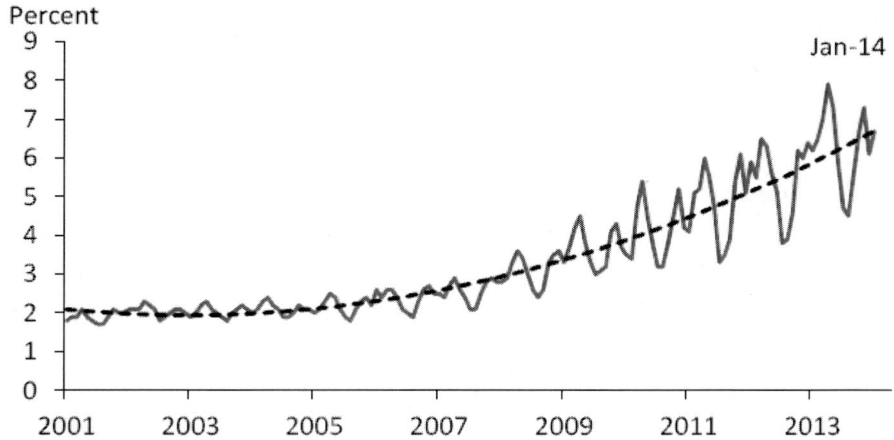

Source: EIA.

Figure 4-6. Monthly Share of Non-Hydro Renewables in Net Power Generation.

The Administration has also supported solar deployment. Five years ago, there were no renewable energy projects on public lands. Today, the Interior Department is on track to permit enough renewable energy projects on public lands by 2020 to power more than six million homes; the Defense Department has set a goal to deploy three gigawatts of renewable energy – including solar, wind, biomass, and geothermal – on Army, Navy, and Air Force installations by 2025; and, as part of the Climate Action Plan, the Federal Government overall has committed to sourcing 20 percent of the energy consumed in Federal buildings from renewable sources by 2020.

Other Renewables

The Administration's All-of-the-Above Energy Strategy also includes other forms of electricity and thermal generation from renewables, including hydropower and geothermal energy. Electricity production from conventional hydropower was 5 percent higher in 2013 than in 2008, although trends in hydropower from year to year depend on water availability. In 2013, President Obama signed two laws aimed at boosting hydropower, in part through encouraging hydropower development at non-powered dams. Similarly, electricity production from geothermal power grew from 2008 to 2013, and the Department of Energy funds research in a number of areas, including enhanced geothermal systems, that hold promise for developing these resources in the future. Finally, the Energy Department funds research in energy storage for applications ranging from better batteries for electric vehicles to energy storage technologies with potential grid-scale applications. Innovations in energy storage can enhance electricity system reliability and resilience, and enable both greater adoption of renewable energy resources and more effective utilization of the existing electric system.

Nuclear and Clean Coal

Nuclear energy provides zero-carbon base load electricity, and through the Energy Department the Administration is supporting nuclear research and deployment. A high priority of the Department has been to help accelerate the timelines for the commercialization and deployment of small modular reactor (SMR) technologies through the SMR Licensing Technical Support program. Small modular reactors offer the advantage of lower initial capital investment, scalability, and siting flexibility at locations unable to accommodate more traditional larger reactors. They also have the potential for enhanced safety and security, for example through built-in passive safety systems. In December 2013, the Energy Department announced an award to support a new project to design, certify and help commercialize SMRs.

The Energy Department is also supporting deployment of advanced large-scale reactors. In February 2014, the Department of Energy issued $6.5 billion in loan guarantees to support the construction of the nation's next generation of advanced nuclear reactors. The two new 1,100- megawatt reactors, which will be located in Georgia, feature advanced safety components and could provide a standardized design for the U.S. utilities market.

The Administration is also advancing clean coal technology. The Department of Energy's clean coal R&D is focused on developing and demonstrating advanced power generation and carbon capture, utilization and storage technologies by increasing overall system efficiencies and reducing capital costs. In the near-term, advanced technologies that increase the power generation efficiency for new plants and technologies to capture CO_2 are being developed. In the longer term, the goal is to increase energy plant efficiencies and reduce both the energy and capital costs of CO_2 capture and storage from new, advanced coal plants and existing plants. As part of its nearly $6 billion commitment to clean coal technology, the Administration, partnered with industry, has already invested in four commercial-scale and 24 industrial-scale CCS projects that together will store more than 15 million metric tons of CO_2

per year and, through oilfield injection, will support production of more than 37.5 million barrels of oil per year.

Meeting the Challenge of the Transportation Sector

Renewables also must play an important role in the transportation sector. Promising low-emission alternatives include hybrids, electric vehicles, hydrogen, natural gas, and biofuels. The effective emissions from an electric vehicle depend on the source of electricity, and will fall as the electric power sector reduces its CO_2 emissions. Different fuels are likely to be relatively better suited for different needs, for example natural gas for busses and heavy-duty fleet vehicles and electricity for private vehicles in urban settings. But the transformation of the transportation sector is in its infancy, so energy policy needs to support research and development of a wide range of advanced transportation fuel options.

The convenience of high energy content liquid fuels means that their role in the transportation sector could persist for decades. If so, renewable liquid fuels with a low GHG footprint would prove important for reducing the climate impact of the transportation sector. Already, the U.S. transportation sector uses ethanol, biodiesel, renewable diesel, and lesser quantities of other renewable fuels. Ethanol is used as a replacement for MTBE to boost octane and is blended into nearly all of the U.S. gasoline supply as E10, which is 10 percent ethanol by volume. Demand for renewable transportation fuels is further supported by the Renewable Fuel Standard (RFS). To qualify under the RFS as conventional renewable fuel, the fuel must achieve a 20 percent life cycle GHG emissions reduction, relative to petroleum gasoline. The legislation authorizing the Renewable Fuel Standard, which was expanded under the Energy Independence and Security Act of 2007, envisioned conventional fuels such as corn ethanol to be transitional and, based on EIA projections at the time, these conventional renewables would constitute a declining share of the total fuel consumption. As Figure 4-7 shows, blending of ethanol into E10 has already reduced the amount of petroleum in gasoline substantially. The long-term environmental goal of the RFS is to support the development of advanced biofuels, which have life cycle GHG emissions reductions of at least 50 percent, and especially to support cellulosic biofuels (which use feedstocks such as corn stover) with GHG emissions reductions of at least 60 percent.

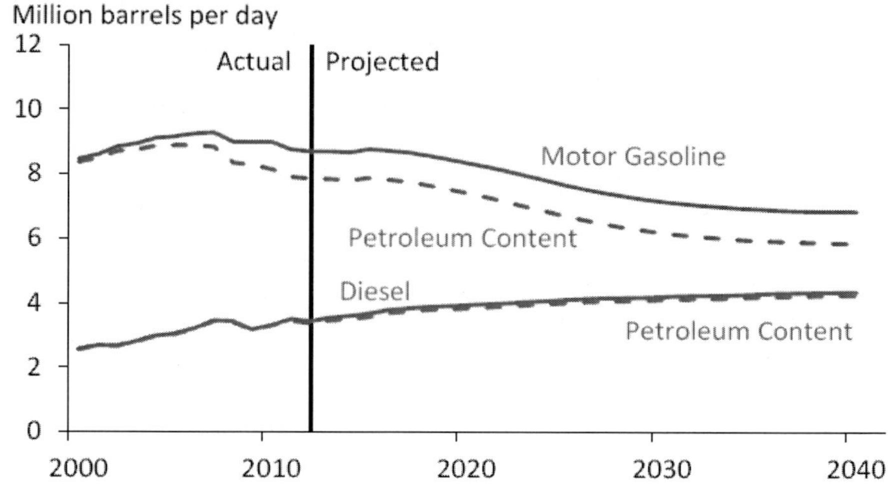

Source: EIA.

Figure 4-7. U.S. Motor Gasoline and Diesel Fuel Consumption, 2000-2040.

International Leadership

From 2005 to 2011 (the last year of data), the United States reduced its total carbon pollution more than any other nation on Earth. The United States is further reducing its GHG emissions through improved energy efficiency, taking advantage of nonconventional natural gas as a transitional fuel, supporting renewable, nuclear, and clean coal energy sources, and regulation under the Clean Air Act. Nevertheless, curbing GHG emissions, like climate change, is ultimately an international challenge. The United States currently produces approximately 15 percent of global carbon emissions, second to China (Figure 4-8). As the economies in the developing world expand, their energy needs will increase, and business-as-usual projections indicate that an increasing share of GHG emissions will come from outside the United States and from the developing world in particular.

While some might suggest that the growing international share of GHG emissions means that U.S. reductions are too small to matter, in fact the opposite is true. U.S. leadership is vital to the success of international negotiations to set meaningful reduction goals. This leadership is multifaceted. Through low-carbon technologies developed and demonstrated in the United States (including nonconventional natural gas technologies), the United States can help the rest of the world reduce its dependence on coal.

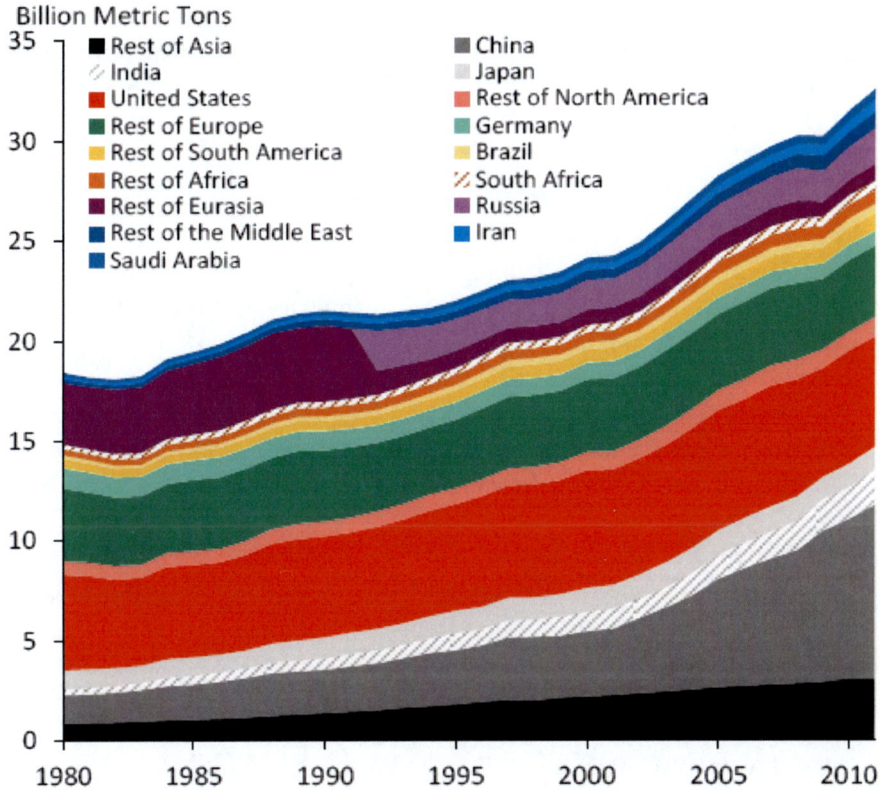

Source: EIA.

Figure 4-8. World Carbon Emissions, 1980-2011.

The President's initiative under the Climate Action Plan to lead efforts to eliminate international public financing for new conventional coal plants, except in the poorest countries without economically feasible alternatives, will further help the world move towards cleaner fuels for electric power. Investing in research in new technologies such as carbon capture and storage for clean coal, natural gas, biomass co-firing, and advanced renewable liquid fuels pushes forward these frontiers, supports U.S. technology leadership in clean energy, and advances technologies that will provide global benefits. And by taking strong steps to reduce emissions at home, through new initiatives such as the second round of heavy duty vehicle fuel economy standards, programs to reduce methane emissions, and regulation of CO2 emissions from fossil fuel fired generators, the Administration is in a much stronger position to secure similar commitments from other nations. The combination of these efforts is laying the foundation for a cleaner energy future that is economically efficient, upholds our responsibility to future generations, and provides positive net economic benefits.

REFERENCES

Barsky, Robert B., and Lutz Kilian. 2002. "Do We Really Know That Oil Caused the Great Stagflation? A Monetary Alternative." *NBER Macroeconomics Annual 2001,* vol. 16, pp. 137–83.

Baumeister, Christiane and Gert Peersman. 2013. "Time-Varying Effects of Oil Supply Shocks on the U.S. Economy." *American Economic Journal: Macroeconomics*, vol. 5, pp. 1-28. Bernanke, Ben S. 1983. "Irreversibility, Uncertainty, and Cyclical Investment." *Quarterly Journal of Economics*, vol. 98, pp. 85-106.

Bernanke, Ben S., Mark Gertler, and Mark Watson. 1997. "Systematic Monetary Policy and the Effects of Oil Price Shocks." *Brookings Papers on Economic Activity,* no. 1: 91–142.

Blanchard, Olivier J., and Jordi Galí. 2010. "The Macroeconomic Effects of Oil Price Shocks: Why Are the 2000s So Different from the 1970s?" In *International Dimensions of Monetary Policy,* edited by Jordi Galí and Mark J. Gertler. University of Chicago Press.

Blinder, Alan. 2009. "Comment on Hamilton, Causes and Consequences of the Oil Shock of 2007-08." *Brookings Papers on Economic Activity*, no. 1: 262-267.

Bloom, Nicholas. 2009. "The Impact of Uncertainty Shocks." *Econometrica* 77:623–85.

Cruz, Jennifer, Peter W. Smith, and Sara Stanley. 2014. "The Marcellus Shale Gas Boom in Pennsylvania: Employment and Wage Trends." *Bureau of Labor Statistics Monthly Labor Review*, February, at http://www.bls.gov/opub/mlr/2014/article/the-marcellus-shalegas-boom-in-pennsylvania.htm

Council of Economic Advisers and Department of Energy. 2013. "Economic Benefits of Increasing Grid Resilience to Weather Outages."

Edelstein, Paul and Lutz Kilian. 2009. "How Sensitive are Consumer Expenditures to Retail Energy?" *Journal of Monetary Economics* 56, 766-779.

Elder, John and Apostolos Serletis. 2010. "Oil Price Uncertainty." *Journal of Money, Credit and Banking*, vol. 42, pp. 1137-1159.

Environmental Protection Agency.2010. "Inventory of U.S. Greenhouse Gas Emissions and Sinks: 1990-2010." (http://www.epa.gov/climatechange /ghgemissions/usinventoryreport.html).

Hamilton, James D. 1983. "Oil and the Macroeconomy since World War II." *Journal of Political Economy* 91, no. 2: 228–48.

Hamilton, James D. 1988. "A Neoclassical Model of Unemployment and the Business Cycle." *Journal of Political Economy* 96, no. 3: 593–617.

Hamilton, James D. 1996. "This Is What Happened to the Oil Price-Macroeconomy Relationship." *Journal of Monetary Economics* 38, no. 2: 215–20.

Hamilton, James D. 2003. "What Is an Oil Shock?" *Journal of Econometrics* 113: 363–98.

Hamilton, James D. 2009. "Causes and Consequences of the Oil Shock of 2007–08." *Brookings Papers on Economic Activity,* no. 1: 215–83.

Hamilton, James D. 2010. "Nonlinearities and the Macroeconomic Effects of Oil Prices." Working Paper no. 16186. Cambridge, Mass.: National Bureau of Economic Research. Hooker, Mark A. 1996. "What Happened to the Oil Price-Macroeconomy Relationship?" *Journal of Monetary Economics* 38: 195-213.

IHS CERA. October 2012. *America's New Energy Future: The Unconventional Oil and Gas Revolution and the U.S. Economy. Volume 1: National Economic Conditions.*

Interagency Working Group on Social Cost of Carbon, United States Government.2010. "Technical Support Document: - Social Cost of Carbon for Regulatory Impact Analysis Under Executive Order 12866".

Jo, Soojin. 2014. "The Effects of Oil Price Uncertainty on Global Real Economic Activity." manuscript, Bank of Canada; forthcoming, *Journal of Money, Credit and Banking*. Kellogg, Ryan. 2010. "The Effect of Uncertainty on Investment: Evidence from Texas Oil Drilling." *NBER Working Paper* 16541.

Kilian, Lutz. 2008a. "Exogenous Oil Supply Shocks: How Big Are They and How Much Do They Matter for the U.S. Economy?" *Review of Economics and Statistics* 90, no. 2: 216–40.

Kilian, Lutz. 2008b. "The Economic Effect of Energy Price Shocks." *Journal of Economic Literature* 46, no. 4: 871–909.

Kilian, Lutz. 2009. "Not All Oil Price Shocks Are Alike: Disentangling Demand and Supply Shocks in the Crude Oil Market." *American Economic Review* 99, no. 3: 1053–69.

Kilian, Lutz. 2014. "Oil Price Shocks: Causes and Consequences." Forthcoming: *Annual Review of Resource Economics.*

Kilian, Lutz and Daniel P. Murphy. 2014. "The Role of Inventories and Speculative Trading in the Global Market for Crude Oil." *Journal of Applied Economics*, vol. 29, pp. 454-478.

Kilian, Lutz and Robert J. Vigfusson. 2014. "The Role of Oil Price Shocks in Causing U.S. Recessions." manuscript, University of Michigan.

Nordhaus, William D. 2007. "Who's Afraid of a Big Bad Oil Shock?" *BPEA,* no. 2:219–238.

Ramey, Valerie A., and Daniel J. Vine. 2010. "Oil, Automobiles, and the U.S. Economy: How Much Have Things Really Changed?" *NBER Macroeconomics Annual* 25: 333–67.

Stock, James H. and Mark W. Watson. 2012. "Disentangling the Channels of the 2007-09 Recession." *Brookings Papers on Economic Activity*, no. 1: 81-135.

End Notes

[1] Throughout the focus is on net imports. Although crude exports are restricted by law and have been historically small quantities, the United States has long exported refined petroleum products, for example averaging approximately 750,000 bpd in the 1990s. Refined product exports have grown sharply since 2006, reaching 2.8 million bpd in 2013.

[2] Estimates of national employment related to the solar energy industry from the Solar Foundation's 2013 National Solar Jobs Census. The National Solar Jobs Census uses a statistical survey methodology aligned with the Bureau of Labor Statistics' Quarterly Census of Employment and Wages and Current Employment Statistics surveys.

[3] Estimates of national employment related to the wind power sector from the 2013 American Wind Energy's Association U.S. Wind Industry Annual Market Report.

[4] The low cost of domestic natural gas relative to other countries reflects the undeveloped nature of international gas markets combined with the expense of transportation. Liquefaction, transportation from the United States to Europe, and regasification have been estimated to add $6-9 per mmBtu, roughly tripling the price of gas entering the pipeline at Europe relative to its Henry Hub price. Currently approximately 9 billion cubic feet per day of liquefied natural gas (LNG) export capacity has been conditionally approved by the Department of Energy, although the enormous capital expenditures required for LNG facilities raises the possibility that some of this capacity might not actually be built. Because of large transport costs, even if a global market for LNG were to develop, domestic natural gas prices are likely to remain well below prices in the rest of the world for an extended period of time.

[5] In a joint statement released May 6, 2014, the G7 energy ministers stated: "We believe that the path to energy security is built on a number of core principles: Development of flexible, transparent and competitive energy markets, including gas markets; Diversification of energy fuels, sources and routes, and encouragement of indigenous sources of energy

supply; Reducing our greenhouse gas emissions, and accelerating the transition to a low carbon economy, as a key contribution to enduring energy security; Enhancing energy efficiency in demand and supply, and demand response management; Promoting deployment of clean and sustainable energy technologies and continued investment in research and innovation; Improving energy systems resilience by promoting infrastructure modernization and supply and demand policies that help withstand systemic shocks; [and] Putting in place emergency response systems, including reserves and fuel substitution for importing countries, in case of major energy disruptions."

6 For example, Kilian and Murphy (2014) estimate the short-run price elasticity of demand for oil to be approximately -0.2, and earlier estimates show even smaller elasticities.

7 The narrow-concept share is available for the full time span, whereas the broader-concept share is available only since 1973. The trend shown in in Figure 3-2 is used to avoid conflating the share with the oil price shock variable with which it is interacted in equation (1).

8 Time series investigations into the macroeconomic effect of oil price volatility using GARCH and/or stochastic volatility approaches include Elder and Serletis (2010) and Jo (2014).

9 The results in Table 3-2 and the corresponding impulse response functions are robust to using instead the autoregressive-distributed lag model with four lags used by Hamilton (2003, 2008), to using a 12-lag distributed lag model (although statistical significance suffers with the added coefficients), to starting the estimation sample in 1954, to ending the estimation sample in 2013, and to using GDP and consumption growth deviated from a longterm cyclically adjusted estimate of their potential growth rates. The estimated impulse response functions are also robust to using instead a bivariate autoregressions with oil ordered causally first as in Edelstein and Kilian (2009), in which the oil price variable is $[ast + (1-a)\mu]pt$ using the estimated value of a reported in Table 3-2.

10 Regulations have costs and benefits, and computing the monetary benefits of reducing CO2 emissions requires an estimate of the net present value of the cost of an additional, or marginal, ton of CO2 emissions. This cost—which covers health, property damage, agricultural impacts, the value of ecosystem services, and other welfare costs of climate change—is often referred to as the "social cost of carbon" (SCC). In 2010, a Federal interagency working group, led by the Council of Economic Advisers and the Office of Management and Budget, produced a white paper that outlined a methodology for estimating the SCC and provided numeric estimates (White House 2010). Since then, the SCC has been used at various stages of rulemaking by the Department of Transportation, the Environmental Protection Agency, and the Department of Energy. The SCC estimate is updated as the science and models underlying the SCC develop, and in November 2013 public comments were invited on the most recent update of the SCC.

11 Specifically, CO2 emissions are the product of (CO2/Btu)×(Btu/GDP)×GDP, where CO2 represents U.S. CO2 emissions in a given year, Btu represents energy consumption in that year, and GDP is that year's GDP. Taking logarithms of this expression, and then subtracting the actual values from the baseline, gives a decomposition of the CO2 reduction into contributions from clean energy, energy efficiency, and the recession.

In: Energy Diversity for Economic Progress ISBN: 978-1-63321-577-1
Editor: Simone Williams

Chapter 2

THE REEMERGENCE OF THE UNITED STATES AS A GLOBAL PETROLEUM PRODUCER*

Edwin Bennion and David Mead

In May 2013, domestic production of petroleum in the United States surpassed imports for the first time since January 1997. The fact that domestic production has outpaced imports is not some random occurrence, but rather the culmination of trends that have been in motion for a number of years. Imports of petroleum have been declining over the last 7 years, while domestic production has undergone a significant revival. According to a forecast by the International Energy Agency, "The United States will overtake Saudi Arabia to become the world's biggest petroleum producer before 2020, and will be energy independent 10 years later."[1]

DECLINE IN U.S. PETROLEUM IMPORTS

In 2005, the amount of foreign crude petroleum and petroleum products imported into the United States peaked at slightly more than 5 billion barrels. Beginning in 2006, the volume of U.S. imports began to decline, and it

* This is an edited, reformatted and augmented version of a U.S. Bureau of Labor Statistics publication, Beyond the Numbers: Global Economy, vol.2, no. 19, issued August 2013.

continued to fall in 6 of the next 7 years. By 2012, imports had declined 22.5 percent, to a little more than 3.8 billion barrels.

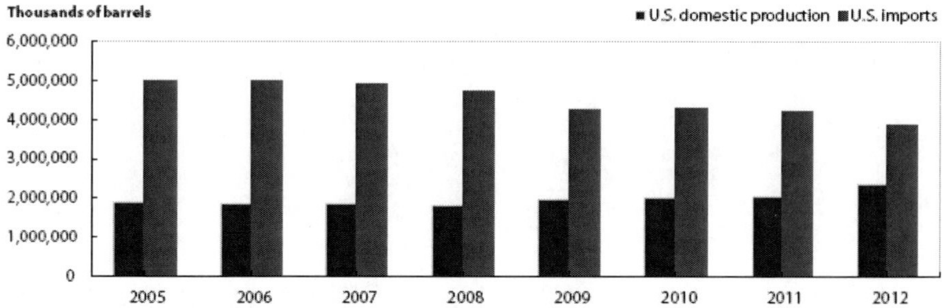

Source: U.S. Energy Information Administration.

Chart 1. U.S. petroleum imports and production, 2005–2012.

As seen in chart 1, 2009 was notable for domestic petroleum production. For the first time in 17 years, U.S. production increased, rising 6.8 percent over the previous year's production, to 1.95 billion barrels. Production continued to expand over the next 3 years and, by 2012, had risen a further 21.7 percent, to 2.38 billion barrels.[2] The increase was particularly evident in 2012, as U.S. production of crude petroleum grew 15.3 percent, well above the global average of 2.2 percent, and averaged 8.9 million barrels of crude petroleum per day.[3] While production in Alaska declined, in the continental United States production grew from a little over 4.7 million barrels per day in 2009 to just under 6 million barrels per day in 2012.[4]

From 2009 to 2012, much of the increase in domestic production came from the rise in crude petroleum production in Texas (87.2 percent), North Dakota (437.4 percent), Oklahoma (39.6 percent), and New Mexico (40.7 percent).[5] The large increases each of those states experienced, some starting as early as 2003, were in stark contrast to the historical trend of declining production that had prevailed nationally since the 1980s. U.S. production grew as a result of new production technologies, such as horizontal drilling and hydraulic fracturing, which were utilized in extracting petroleum and gas from shale deposits once viewed as unprofitable.[6]

With the overall increase in domestic production came an expansion in the amount of drilling activity. The number of rotary rigs (the machinery used to drill petroleum wells) in operation rose considerably from 2002 to 2011. In 2002, there were 137 rotary rigs in operation in the United States. By 2011, the number had grown 618.2 percent, to 984.[7] There was also an increase in the number of petroleum wells in the nation: from 1997 to 2002, the number of active petroleum wells had declined 9.1 percent, but from 2002 to 2009, the number grew from 354,640 to 363,459, an increase of 2.5 percent. [8]

Coinciding with the large increase in domestic petroleum production in the United States was a decline in the domestic consumption of petroleum. Domestic petroleum consumption fell from 18.9 million barrels a day in 2011 to 18.6 million barrels per day in 2012, a decrease of 1.6 percent.[9] The amount of petroleum consumed in 2012 was the smallest since 1996.

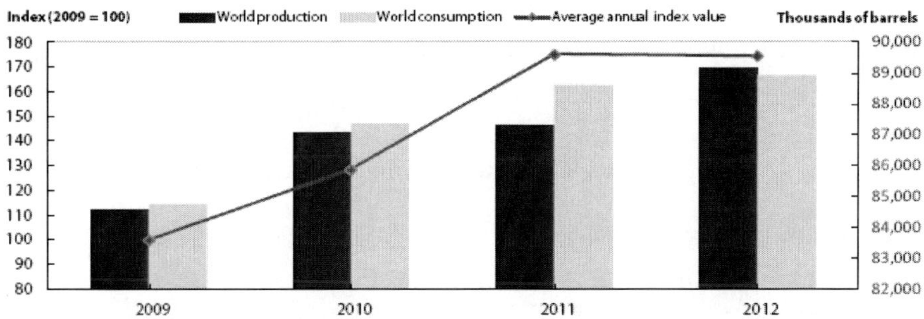

Source: Price Indexes from U.S Bureau of Labor Statistics; petroleum production and consumption data from U.S. Energy Information Administration.

Chart 2. U.S. petroleum import price index and world petroleum production and consumption, 2009–2012.

The decline in demand manifested itself in the major economic sectors. The most important sector of the U.S. economy in terms of petroleum usage is the transportation sector. At the height of consumption in 2007, 14.3 million barrels of petroleum were consumed per day, with 9.1 million barrels per day going toward the production of gasoline. By 2012, gasoline consumption had decreased 6.6 percent, to 8.5 million barrels per day. Overall consumption in the transportation sector, which accounted for 70.5 percent of total U.S. petroleum consumption, declined 9.1 percent, to 13 million barrels per day, the lowest annual figure since 2001.[10] Part of the decrease in consumption was brought about by a decline in vehicle distance traveled by American drivers. By 2012, the number of miles driven by Americans was 2.5 percent less than in 2008.[11] At the same time, the vehicles being driven became more fuel efficient. The U.S. Environmental Protection Agency reported that the estimated composite average fuel economy of 2012 model-year cars and trucks was 23.8 mpg, the highest mileage since the EPA began publishing the figure in 1975.[12]

Decreasing consumption in the industrial, residential, and commercial sectors also contributed to the overall decline in domestic consumption of petroleum. The U.S. recession, which began in 2008, was an important contributor to the decline in both the industrial and the residential sector's consumption of petroleum. Domestic industrial petroleum consumption fell 10.9 percent from 2008 to 2012, while residential consumption dropped 15.0 percent. Commercial consumption decreased 2.5 percent. One of the contributors to the decline in residential petroleum consumption is the construction of housing that is more energy efficient than previously; the amount of energy used to heat new houses has decreased.[13]

Import Petroleum Prices

While the volume of petroleum imports to the United States started to decline as early as 2006 and domestic production began increasing in 2009, the price index for imported petroleum continued to rise until 2012. (See chart 2.) Several factors helped keep import prices rising until 2012. Strong global demand, especially from Asia; lower production from several nations that are members of the Organization of the Petroleum Exporting Countries (OPEC);[14] and global supply shocks all contributed to increasing prices. By 2012, the growth in production worldwide, coupled with steadying global demand, started to drive prices down.

In 2010, import prices for petroleum rose 28.4 percent over the 2009 figure, on the strength of robust global demand; demand from Asia was particularly strong. Consumption in Asia grew 6.0 percent in 2010, while global consumption increased 3.1 percent.[15] Much of the increase in consumption came from China, which experienced record demand during the year.

The rise in import petroleum prices (36.4 percent) was even more pronounced in 2011. Both supply concerns resulting from political unrest in North Africa and strong worldwide demand contributed to the higher prices. The political unrest began with protests against the Egyptian government. Although Egypt is a relatively small producer of petroleum, fears that the turmoil might lead to disruptions in the traffic of petroleum passing through the Suez Canal helped drive prices higher. The political unrest continued with a civil war that broke out in neighboring Libya in February, producing uncertainty that contributed to a worldwide rise in petroleum prices. As a result, Libyan petroleum exports fell from more than 1.5 million barrels a day before the crisis to 200,000 barrels a day by April.[16] Strong demand from Asian countries continued into 2011 as Asian consumption increased 3.6 percent and Chinese consumption grew 5.2 percent.[17]

After 2 consecutive years of sizable increases, import prices leveled off in 2012, falling 0.3 percent for the year. Petroleum prices rose during the first quarter of 2012, but then fell 13.2 percent from March to December. Contributing to the price decline were increases in production by Russia, Canada, and the OPEC nations. Of particular note, the United States increased production by more than 15 percent, the largest single-year rise since the 18.9–percent hike in 1940.[18] While global production was rising, the growth in world consumption of petroleum slowed in 2012, ticking up 0.4 percent.[19]

THE CHANGING FACE OF THE U.S. PETROLEUM SUPPLY

3The recent surge in U.S. petroleum production, coupled with reduced growth in energy consumption, has lessened the nation's reliance on petroleum imports and caused a historical shift in the U.S. energy outlook. Though certainly a positive development for the United States, this shift is expected to have global implications as well. In its most recent *Medium-Term Oil Market Report*, the International Energy Agency stated that the boom in North American petroleum production will ease what has been a tight market and reshape market fundamentals.[20] The North American supply is forecasted to expand by 3.9 million barrels per day over the next 6 years, helping offset potential market disruptions from volatile regions such as the Middle East.

CURRENT PRICE TRENDS: SECOND QUARTER, 2013, HIGHLIGHTS

Import Prices

U.S. import prices fell 1.6 percent in the second quarter of 2013, after increasing 1.3 percent over the first quarter. A downturn in fuel prices was one factor in the second-quarter decrease in import prices. Also contributing to the decline were lower nonfuel prices, led by a 1.6-percent drop in import prices from Japan. The decrease in prices of imports from Japan paralleled the rise in the value of the U.S. dollar relative to the yen: the dollar rose 14.5 percent against the yen over the first half of 2013. The decline in the price index for imports from Japan is the largest quarterly drop in the index since 1998.

Fuel imports. Fuel prices fell 4.1 percent over the second quarter of 2013, following a 5.6-percent increase in the index for the first quarter of the year. The second-quarter drop resulted from a 1.9-percent decline in fuel prices in May and a 2.4-percent decrease in April. In contrast, prices for import fuels ticked up 0.1 percent in June. The second-quarter decline in fuel prices was led by a 4.7-percent decrease in petroleum prices, more than offsetting a 15.6-percent increase in natural gas prices.

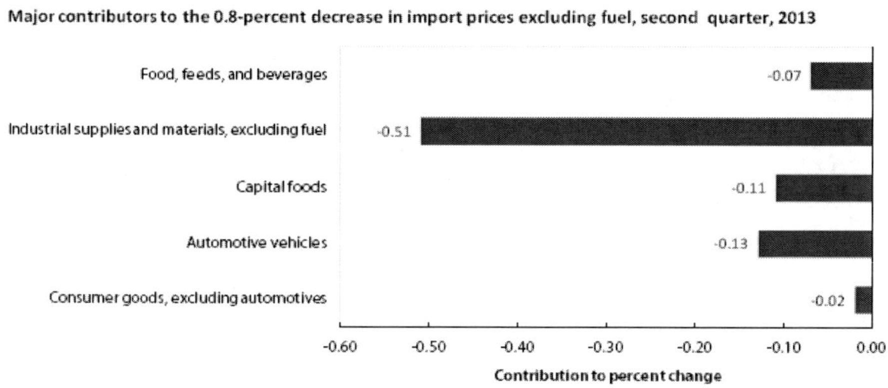

Note: Because of rounding, figures do not sum to total.
Source: U.S. Bureau of Labor Statistics.

Chart 3. Major contributors to the 0.8-percent decrease in import prices excluding fuel, second quarter, 2013.

The second-quarter decrease in petroleum prices followed a 6.2-percent increase during the first quarter and resumed the overall downward trend in the price of this commodity throughout 2012, when petroleum prices fell 8.7 percent. As indicated earlier, strong world supply and weakened demand contributed to the drop in petroleum prices. Another factor was the rising value of the U.S. dollar against most major currencies in recent months. Petroleum is generally priced in U.S. dollars, so a stronger dollar makes petroleum prices more expensive (thus weakening demand) for countries using other currencies to purchase petroleum.

In contrast to petroleum prices, the price index for natural gas rose 15.6 percent between March and June, resulting mostly from a 15.5-percent jump in April. Prices for natural gas increased 93.3 percent over the past year. The low price level in 2012 led to some cutback in production because profit levels became unsustainable as a result of the reduced prices.[21]

Nonfuel imports. Nonfuel import prices fell 0.8 percent between March and June, after ticking up 0.2 percent over the first quarter of 2013. The decrease was the largest quarterly decline since the index fell 1.8 percent over the first quarter of 2009.

As seen by the contributions shown in chart 3, the second-quarter decline was driven primarily by falling prices for nonfuel industrial supplies and materials, which dropped 3.0 percent. That decrease followed a 0.1-percent advance between December 2012 and March 2013, and was led by a 7.5-percent drop in prices for unfinished metals. Prices for gold and other precious metals have fallen because of smaller demand from investors on lessening fears of inflation.[22]

Each of the major finished goods areas recorded declines over the second quarter of 2013, in part because of the rising value of the U.S. dollar. Prices for automotive vehicles fell 0.9 percent for the quarter ended in June, the largest quarterly decrease in the index since a 1.0-percent drop in June 1991. Capital goods prices declined 0.3 percent between March and June: the most recent quarter that this index increased was the third quarter of 2012. The price index for consumer goods also decreased in the second quarter, edging down 0.1 percent.

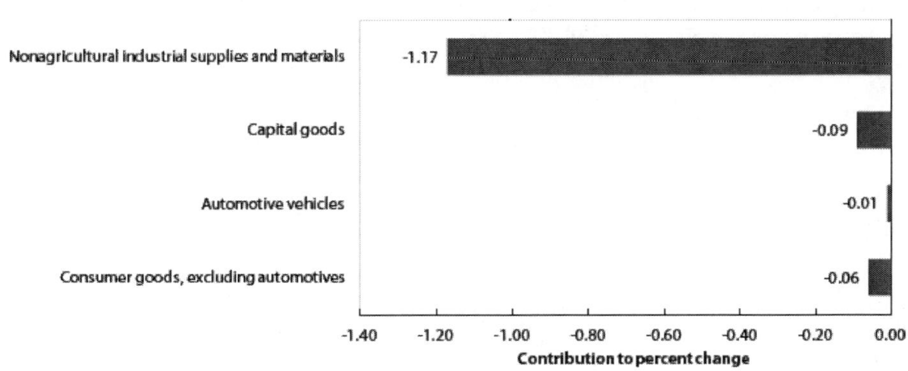

Note: Because of rounding, figures do not sum to total.
Source: U.S. Bureau of Labor Statistics.

Chart 4. Major contributors to the 1.4-percent decrease in export prices excluding agriculture, second quarter, 2013.

Prices for foods, feeds, and beverages fell for the quarter ended in June, decreasing 1.1 percent, after a 2.7-percent increase over the previous 3 months. A 5.4-percent decline in vegetable prices, a 7.4-percent drop in coffee prices, and a 3.1-percent decrease in fruit prices offset higher prices for fish and shellfish in the second quarter.

Export Prices

Overall export prices decreased 1.3 percent in the second quarter of 2013, following a 0.6-percent increase the previous quarter. Both agricultural prices and nonagricultural prices contributed to the decline. The March-to-June drop in export prices was the largest quarterly decline since a 1.8-percent decrease in the second quarter of 2012.

Agricultural exports. The price index for agricultural exports fell 0.6 percent for the second quarter of 2013, entirely attributable to a 2.3-percent drop in April. Following the April decline, prices for U.S agricultural exports rose 1.7 percent over the remainder of the quarter. A 4.1-percent drop in corn prices for the 3 months ended in June was the largest contributor to the falling agricultural prices and was driven by an 8.1-percent decrease in April corn prices. Prices for export corn fell 5.5 percent during the first quarter of 2013. The drop was due to higher than originally estimated stockpiles and to forecasts that the acreage planted this year might be the largest since 1936.[23] However, corn prices reversed direction in May and June, rising 4.5 percent over those months as rainy weather in much of the corn-growing region of the United States led to late planting. As of April 28, only about 5 percent of the U.S. corn crop was in the ground.[24]

Lower prices for nuts and cotton in the second quarter of 2013 also factored into the overall decline in agricultural export prices.

Nonagricultural exports. Nonagricultural export prices declined 1.4 percent between March and June, after rising 0.8 percent over the first quarter of the year. As seen in chart 4, most of the decrease resulted from prices for nonagricultural industrial supplies and materials, which fell 3.2 percent for the quarter. A 5.2-percent decline in fuel prices and a 9.5-percent decrease in prices for nonferrous metals were the two largest contributors to the overall drop in prices for nonagricultural industrial supplies and materials.

Each of the major finished goods areas recorded comparatively modest price declines for the quarter ended in June: consumer goods prices fell 0.5 percent, prices for capital goods decreased 0.3 percent, and the price index for export automotive vehicles edged down 0.1 percent.

End Notes

[1] Mark Thompson, "U.S. to become biggest oil producer–IEA," CNN Money, November 12, 2012, http://money.cnn.com/2012/11/12/news/economy/us-oil-production-energy/ index. html.

[2] "Crude Oil Production," Petroleum & Other Liquids (U.S. Energy Information Administration, March 15, 2013), http://www.eia.gov/dnav/pet/pet_crd_crpdn_adc_mbbl_a.htm.

[3] "BP Statistical Review of World Energy June 2013" BP, http://www.bp.com/content/ dam/bp/pdf/statistical-review/ statistical_review_of_world_energy_2013.pdf.

[4] "July 2013 Monthly Energy Review" (U.S. Energy Information Administration, July 26, 2013), table 3.1, http://www.eia.gov/ totalenergy/data/monthly/pdf/mer.pdf.

[5] "Crude Oil Production."

[6] "U.S. oil production in largest ever single-year increase," BBC News Business, June 12, 2013, http://www.bbc.co.uk/news/ business-22875526.

[7] "Crude Oil and Natural Gas Drilling Activity," Petroleum & Other Liquids (U.S. Energy Information Administration, September 7, 2012), http://www.eia.gov/dnav/pet/pet_crd_ drill_s1_a.htm.

[8] "Distribution and Production of Oil and Gas Wells by State" (U.S. Energy Information Administration, January 7, 2011), http://www.eia.gov/pub/oil_gas/petrosystem/ petrosysog. html; 2009 is the last year for which published data are available.

[9] "Total Petroleum Consumption" (U.S. Energy Information Administration, June 27, 2013), http://www.eia.gov/cfapps/ ipdbproject/IEDIndex3.cfm?tid=5&pid=5&aid=2.

[10] "July 2013 Monthly Energy Review," table 3.7c.

[11] "Traffic Volume Trends," Travel Monitoring (U.S. Department of Transportation, Federal Highway Administration, May 2013), http://www.fhwa.dot.gov/policyinformation/travel_ monitoring/tvt.cfm.

[12] "Light-Duty Automotive Technology, Carbon Dioxide Emissions, and Fuel Economy Trends: 1975 Through 2012," Cars and Light Trucks (United States Environmental Protection Agency, March 21, 2013), http://www.epa.gov/otaq/fetrends.htm#report.

[13] "Newer U.S. homes are 30% larger but consume about as much energy as older homes," Today in Energy (U.S. Energy Information Administration, February 12, 2013), http://www.eia.gov/todayinenergy/detail.cfm?id=9951. OPEC member nations are Algeria, Angola, Ecuador, Iran, Iraq, Kuwait, Libya,

[14] Nigeria, Qatar, Saudi Arabia, United Arab Emirates, and Venezuela.

[15] "BP Statistical Review of World Energy"; and "International Energy Statistics" (U.S. Energy Information Agency), http://www.eia.gov/ cfapps/ipdbproject/IEDIndex3.cfm.

[16] "Oil Market Report" (International Energy Agency, May 12, 2011), omrpublic.iea.org/ omrarchive/12may11full.pdf.

[17] "BP Statistical Review of World Energy."

[18] "Crude Oil Production."

[19] "Total Petroleum Consumption."

[20] "Supply shock from North American oil rippling through global markets" (International Energy Agency, May 14, 2013), http://www.iea.org/newsroomandevents/pressreleases/2013/may/name,38080,en.html.

[21] Erich Schwartzel, "U.S. report predicts rising natural gas prices in 2013–14," Pittsburgh Post-Gazette, January 9, 2013, http://www.post-gazette.com/stories/business/news/us-report-predicts-rising-natural-gas-prices-in-2013-14-669602.

[22] Jan Harvey, "Gold hits two-and-half year low as Fed flags end to easy money," Reuters, June 20, 2013, http://news.yahoo.com/ gold-hits-two-half-low-fed-flags-end-161417771.html.

[23] "Corn Heads for Bear Market After U.S. Stockpiles Beat Estimates," Agweb, April 1, 2013, http://www.agweb.com/article/ corn_heads_for_bear_market_after_us_stockpiles_ beat_ estimates.

[24] "April Showers (and Snow) Bring Market Chaos," Agweb, May 1, 2013, http://www.agweb .com/mobile/ newsdetail.aspx?ArticleId=334963.

In: Energy Diversity for Economic Progress
Editor: Simone Williams
ISBN: 978-1-63321-577-1

Chapter 3

ENERGY POLICY: 113TH CONGRESS ISSUES*

Carl E. Behrens

SUMMARY

Energy policy in the United States has focused on three major goals: assuring a secure supply of energy, keeping energy costs low, and protecting the environment. In pursuit of those goals, government programs have been developed to improve the efficiency with which energy is utilized, to promote the domestic production of conventional energy sources, and to develop new energy sources, particularly renewable sources.

Implementing these programs has been controversial because of varying importance given to different aspects of energy policy. For some, dependence on imports of foreign oil, particularly from the Persian Gulf, is the primary concern; for others, the indiscriminate use of fossil fuels, whatever their origin, is most important. The contribution of burning fossil fuels to global climate change is particularly controversial. Another dichotomy is between those who see government intervention as a positive force and those who view it as a necessary evil at best.

The 112th Congress did not take up comprehensive energy legislation, but numerous bills were considered on specific energy issues. The most significant action was extension of energy tax incentives, including the Production Tax Credit (PTC) for wind energy, to January 1,

* This is an edited, reformatted and augmented version of a Congressional Research Service publication R42756, prepared for Members and Committees of Congress, dated March 21, 2014.

2014, as part of P.L. 112-240, The American Taxpayer Relief Act of 2012. With the expiration of the extension, the issue of the PTC is once again an issue before Congress.

In the 113th Congress, a number of issues, some of which drew attention previously, have been taken up in proposed legislation. The Energy Savings and Industrial Competitiveness Act of 2013, S. 1392 and H.R. 1616, would promote energy efficiency in buildings and industry by encouraging adoption of uniform building codes and authorize a grant program for state energy efficiency programs. The bill was reported out by the Senate Energy and Natural Resources Committee on May 13, 2013, but attempts to bring it to the Senate floor failed. The bill was reintroduced with some amendments as S. 2074 in March 2014, and on March 5 the House passed H.R. 2126, which contains some of the provisions in S. 2074, by a vote of 375-36.

H.R. 3, the Northern Route Approval Act, would declare that a presidential permit would not be required for construction of the Keystone XL pipeline from Canada to the Gulf of Mexico. The bill passed the House on May 22, 2013, by a vote of 241-175. The issue of approving the Keystone XL pipeline is deeply involved in the question of global climate change, since opponents argue that Canadian oil sands production contributes excessive amounts of greenhouse gas emissions.

In November 2013 the House passed three energy related bills. H.R. 2728 would prohibit the Bureau of Land Management from enforcing rules to regulate hydraulic fracturing in any state that has its own regulations on the activity. H.R. 1900 would require the Federal Energy Regulatory Commission to respond to permit applications for new natural gas pipelines within one year. H.R. 1965 would be aimed at increasing on-shore leasing of oil and gas resources on federal land. On March 6, 2014, the House passed H.R. 3826, a bill to block the Environmental Protection Agency from limiting power plant carbon emissions.

INTRODUCTION

U.S. energy policy since the Arab oil embargo in the 1970s has been aimed at a long-term goal with three major dimensions: to assure a secure supply of energy, to keep energy costs low enough to meet the needs of a growing economy, and to protect the environment while producing and consuming that energy. A continuing theme during this period has been that dependence on imported oil for a large share of the U.S. energy mix, particularly in the transportation sector, impedes that aim in all three dimensions. But the importance given to import dependence varies. For some, import dependence is the primary concern; for others, particularly those focused on environmental issues, it is a symptom of a general crisis that arises from indiscriminate consumption of fossil fuels. A particularly controversial aspect of the debate is the issue of global climate change, because burning fossil fuels produces large amounts of carbon dioxide, a greenhouse gas.

Like the goals of energy policy, the means of achieving them have three dimensions: reducing consumption by increased energy efficiency; increasing domestic production of conventional energy sources, particularly oil; and developing new sources of energy, particularly renewable energy and renewable fuels, that can replace oil and other fossil fuels.

Pursuing the goals of energy policy has been complicated by the diversity of energy consumption and supply in the United States. On the consumption side, there are three major sectors: residential/commercial, industrial, and transportation. On the supply side, the primary sources have traditionally been fossil energy: petroleum, natural gas (and "natural gas liquids" such as propane and butane), and coal. Electricity, which is both an energy source and a consumer of energy, has replaced some fossil fuels: about 75% of the energy consumed by the residential/commercial sector is electricity, and industrial energy consumption is about 35% electricity. But in the transportation sector, petroleum has remained dominant. Only in the past few years has corn-derived ethanol become a significant transportation fuel, replacing close to 10% of gasoline consumption.

A diverse spectrum of generating sources is used to produce electricity. Coal for many years supplied half the electricity generated nationally. In recent years its share has declined; it was about 40% in December 2013. Generation by natural gas has risen in importance, supplying about 26% in December 2013. To those who regard global climate change as an urgent issue, this trend is important because generating electricity from coal emits roughly twice the carbon dioxide per kilowatt-hour than generating from natural gas. Nuclear fission supplies about 20%, hydropower less than 10%. Petroleum, an important generating fuel in the 1970s and early 1980s, now contributes less than 1% of electricity generation. A surge of construction of wind-powered generating capacity has brought its share of total generation to almost 5%.

An issue that cuts across all these factors is the role of government. How much does government policy affect energy markets? A fundamental dichotomy that lies beneath many individual policy debates, not only in energy issues, is between those who see government intervention as a positive force, and those who view it at best as a necessary evil to be restricted as much as possible.

POLICY GOALS

Conservation and Energy Efficiency

Reducing energy consumption by conservation and by increased efficiency of energy use has been a major component of policy since the first energy crisis in the 1970s. Most prominent has been setting fuel economy standards for automobiles and trucks.[1] Federal research and development programs in energy-efficient technologies have had continued support over many years, pursuing improvements in building technology, in industrial processes, and in vehicle efficiency—the last including battery designs that have been used in producing hybrid vehicles.[2] Development of "Smart Grid" technologies in electric power distribution systems to encourage more efficient use of electricity has received much recent attention. Grant programs to improve and "weatherize" existing residences have received continued funding, but like all such programs they have become controversial in the current tight budget environment.[3] Standards for home appliances such as air conditioners, refrigerators, and washing machines are another policy program that has had continued support, and some controversy. A requirement to raise efficiency levels in light bulbs has been an issue for several years.

Increasing Domestic Supply Production of Oil

With dependence on oil imports probably the most high-profile energy policy issue, the question of domestic oil production has a long history of controversy. Much exploration and development of new oil resources involves federal land, particularly on the outer continental shelf (OCS) and in Alaska, and environmental concerns have led to extended moratoria on leasing for many areas.[4] The Deepwater Horizon oil spill in the Gulf of Mexico in 2010 added a further dimension to the question of OCS leasing.[5] In recent years, development of Canadian oil sands resources, and of tight oil deposits in the United States, has added further controversy over the possible environmental effects of their production and transportation.[6] The proposed Keystone XL pipeline to bring Canadian crude to Texas refineries has been particularly controversial.[7]

In addition, for some, increasing production of oil is in principle to be avoided, since it merely postpones the replacement of fossil fuels by renewable energy and makes the transition more difficult. Others are particularly opposed to development of oil sands, on the grounds that it produces more greenhouse gases than conventional oil production.[8]

The Price of Oil and Gasoline

Since 2004, oil and gasoline markets have been highly volatile. Throughout this period some have argued that prices were being driven not by the cost of producing the resources but by speculation and unregulated manipulation of the markets. The Dodd-Frank Wall Street Reform Act of 2010 (P.L. 111-203) aimed to address these concerns, but its application and enforcement remain controversial.[9] The issue is complicated because oil prices are largely determined in a world market beyond the reach of domestic regulation.

An additional issue involving oil and gasoline prices is the role of the Strategic Petroleum Reserve (SPR), which was set up after the Arab oil embargoes to fill temporary interruptions in the supply of oil. In principle releases from the SPR are limited to cases in which a physical lack of supply exists, but some have argued that it can be used to dampen surges in world oil prices even when current supply is adequate to meet demand. The June 2011 release of 30 million barrels from the SPR in response to the Libyan civil war has been deemed by some critics as such an attempt to influence the market when U.S. supplies were adequate.[10]

Natural Gas

Unlike the world oil market, in which events abroad quickly affect prices locally, the natural gas market is largely domestic. Except for about 5% net imports from Canada by pipeline, 2012 gas consumption, 25.5 trillion cubic feet, was almost entirely produced in the United States. Production since 2010 has increased sharply, largely as a result of development of tight shale formations. As with tight oil production, shale gas development has brought environmental concerns about the effects on ground water of hydraulic fracturing. The need for gathering infrastructure and pipeline construction from new fields is also an issue.

With gas production up and demand not growing as quickly, the likelihood of increasing exports of liquefied natural gas (LNG) has increased. LNG requires complex and expensive processing and loading facilities that have been controversial in locations where they have been proposed. There is also the prospect of controversy over the question of exporting energy resources such as natural gas, and its effect on prices and supply.[11]

Electric Power Production

The electric power sector since the mid-1980s has been essentially independent of the major energy policy issue of dependence on imported oil, since oil-generated electricity is a very small part of the generation mix. Nevertheless, electricity's central role in America's energy mix makes it subject to numerous controversies.

A major consideration is the role of the coal industry. More than 1 billion tons of coal are consumed in the United States each year, about 93% of it burned to produce electricity. Initiatives by the Environmental Protection Agency (EPA) that would impose tighter emissions restrictions on coal-fired power plants are particularly controversial. Limits on cross-state emissions of sulfur dioxide and nitrogen oxides, emissions of mercury and other hazardous pollutants, and regulation of greenhouse gas emissions, among other proposed regulations, have been characterized by critics as a regulatory "train wreck" that would impose excessive costs and lead to plant retirements that could threaten the adequacy of electricity capacity (i.e., reliability of supply) across the country, although some in the electric power industry consider those concerns overstated.[12]

Nuclear power is also a continuing issue. Although subject to continuing opposition over questions of safety, disposal of radioactive waste, and possible proliferation of nuclear weapons, nuclear fission has gained support because it does not emit greenhouse gases. However, cost considerations in the face of increasing natural gas production, and safety concerns enhanced by the tsunami-caused accident at Japan's Fukushima nuclear plant in March 2011, have put further expansion of nuclear power in question.[13]

Replacing Conventional Energy Sources

The third path toward reaching the goals of energy policy is to develop alternative sources of energy to replace fossil fuels. As noted, reducing the need for imported oil has been a major feature of energy policy, and congressional mandates have led to increased consumption of ethanol.

However, essentially all fuel ethanol currently is produced from corn, potentially putting pressure on food production and food prices. The technology for producing ethanol from nonfood sources (including cellulosic biomass) faces serious technological barriers. Another transportation alternative, long considered but only slowly adopted, has been natural gas-powered vehicles. Recent increases in natural gas production, noted above, have made this option appear more attractive, although developing a supply infrastructure and overcoming technological and cost difficulties continue to present barriers to widespread adoption.

For many participants in the energy debate, replacing fossil fuels has been a goal not limited to the transportation sector, however. Electricity production by renewable energy sources—wind power, concentrating solar power, photovoltaic cells, geothermal energy, biomass—is the goal of many initiatives: research and development programs, tax benefits, loan guarantees, and mandates.

The main stimulus for these programs is environmental, including concern about global climate change, but the prospect of developing new industrial production from expansion of renewable energy sources has been a significant, if controversial, theme. Even nuclear power, long a target of environmental concerns, has been considered a viable alternative to fossil energy for electricity generation, although once again the influx of newly developed natural gas resources has raised serious questions about the cost competitiveness of new nuclear power generators.

ENERGY LEGISLATION

Energy policy historically has been legislated mostly in large, complex bills that deal with a wide variety of issues, with debate spanning several sessions. The Energy Policy Act of 2005 (EPAct 2005; P.L. 109-58) was the most recent comprehensive general legislation, with provisions and authorizations in almost all areas of energy policy. EPAct 2005 also set up in DOE the program of energy project loan guarantees which has become a source of controversy and debate following the bankruptcy of the Solyndra solar system manufacturing facility in 2011.[14]

The Energy Independence and Security Act of 2007 (EISA, P.L. 110-140) set new target fuel economy standards for cars and light trucks of 35 miles per gallon by 2020, and increased the renewable fuels standard (RFS) to start at 9.0 billion gallons in 2008 and rise to 36 billion gallons by 2022. EISA also included new efficiency standards for appliances and for light bulbs, the latter being particularly controversial in the 112th Congress.

In the 111th Congress the American Recovery and Reinvestment Act (the "Stimulus" Act, ARRA, P.L. 111-5) had major energy policy provisions, including expansion of the loan guarantee program and large increases in funding for renewable energy programs. The Office of Energy Efficiency and Renewable Energy programs, in addition to the $2 billion appropriated in the FY2009 regular appropriations bill, received $17 billion in ARRA, of which $11.5 billion was for grants to states for energy, efficiency, and weatherization programs. The Office of Electricity Delivery and Energy Reliability, which had historically been funded at about $150 million per year, received $4.5 billion in ARRA, directed at establishing "Smart Grid" technology for the electric power industry.

Legislation in the 112th and 113th Congress

The 112th Congress did not deal with major energy legislation, but numerous energy policy questions were taken up in proposed legislation. The major action was passage of the "fiscal cliff" act: P.L. 112-240, The American Taxpayer Relief Act of 2012, signed into law January 2, 2013. It was primarily concerned with averting scheduled income tax rate increases and spending reductions required by the Budget Control Act (P.L. 112-25), but it included temporary extension of certain energy tax provisions. Specifically, the Production Tax Credit (PTC) for wind was extended through January 1, 2014. For all PTC-eligible technologies, the placed-in-service deadline was replaced with a construction start date. Other expired energy tax incentives, including several incentives for biofuels and alternative fuels, as well as incentives for certain types of energy-efficient property, were also extended.[15] With the expiration of the extension, the PTC and other energy tax provisions are again issues before Congress.[16]

In the 113th Congress, the following issues have attracted legislative attention.

Keystone XL Pipeline and Other Pipeline Legislation

In the ongoing debate over approval of the proposed Keystone XL pipeline to bring Canadian oil sands crude oil to the Gulf of Mexico, H.R. 3, the Northern Route Approval Act, would declare that a presidential permit would not be required for its construction.[17] The bill passed the House on May 22, 2013, by a vote of 241-175.

In response to the wide spread of new production of natural gas and a consequent pressure to expand the means of transporting it to market, the House passed legislation (H.R. 1900) on November 21, 2013, to require the Federal Energy Regulatory Administration (FERC) to respond to new gas pipeline permit applications within one year.[18]

Increasing Domestic Production

A bill to increase on-shore leasing of oil and gas resources on federal land (H.R. 1965), including the National Petroleum Reserve in Alaska, and shale oil deposits in Colorado, passed the House on November 21, 2013.

Regulation of Power Plant Emissions and Global Climate Change

As noted above, EPA's moves to regulate emissions from coal-fired power plants have been controversial, and several bills in the 112th Congress passed the House without being taken up in the Senate.

On June 25, 2013, President Obama announced a national plan to reduce emissions of carbon dioxide and other greenhouse gases, as well as to encourage adaptation to expected climate change. A major feature of the President's Climate Action Plan was a directive to the Environmental Protection Agency to issue rules to curtail carbon dioxide emissions from new and existing power plants.[19] On March 6, 2014, the House passed H.R. 3826, a bill to block the Environmental Protection Agency from limiting power plant carbon emissions, by a vote of 229- 183.

Hydraulic Fracturing

The issue of regulation and safety of hydraulic fracturing led to differing legislative proposals. Under provisions of EPAct 2005, EPA does not have regulatory jurisdiction over certain aspects of hydraulic fracturing. In the 112th Congress, one proposed legislative solution, the Fracturing Responsibility and Awareness of Chemicals Act (FRAC Act, H.R. 1084 and S. 587), would have given EPA such jurisdiction under the Safe Drinking Water Act. Another bill would have maintained jurisdiction within the states. Neither legislative proposal was reported out of committee. In the 113th Congress, the FRAC Act was reintroduced as H.R. 1921.

Another aspect of the hydraulic fracturing issue is the proposal by the Bureau of Land Management (BLM) to regulate fracking on federal lands.[20] On November 20, 2013, the House passed H.R. 2728, which would prohibit the Department of the Interior from enforcing rules related to hydraulic fracturing in "any state that has regulations, guidance or permit requirements for that activity."

Energy Efficiency

The Energy Savings and Industrial Competitiveness Act of 2013, S. 1392 and H.R. 1616, would promote energy efficiency in buildings and industry by encouraging adoption of uniform building codes and authorize a grant program for state energy efficiency programs. The bill was reported out by the Senate Energy and Natural Resources Committee on May 13, 2013, but attempts to bring it to the Senate floor failed.[21] The bill was reintroduced with some amendments as S. 2074 in March 2014, and on March 5 the House passed H.R. 2126, which contains some of the provisions in S. 2074, by a vote of 375-36.

End Notes

[1] For details, see CRS Report R42721, Automobile and Truck Fuel Economy (CAFE) and Greenhouse Gas Standards, by Brent D. Yacobucci, Bill Canis, and Richard K. Lattanzio.

[2] See CRS Report R42498, Energy and Water Development: FY2013 Appropriations, coordinated by Carl E. Behrens.

[3] See CRS Report R42147, DOE Weatherization Program: A Review of Funding, Performance, and Cost-Effectiveness Studies, by Fred Sissine.

[4] See CRS Report R42432, U.S. Crude Oil and Natural Gas Production in Federal and Non-Federal Areas, by Marc Humphries, and CRS Report R41132, Outer Continental Shelf Moratoria on Oil and Gas Development, by Curry L. Hagerty.

[5] See CRS Report R41684, Enacted and Proposed Oil Spill Legislation in the 112th Congress, by Jonathan L. Ramseur.

[6] See CRS Report R41760, Hydraulic Fracturing and Safe Drinking Water Act Regulatory Issues, by Mary Tiemann and Adam Vann.

[7] See CRS Report R41668, Keystone XL Pipeline Project: Key Issues, by Paul W. Parfomak et al., and CRS Report R42611, Oil Sands and the Keystone XL Pipeline: Background and Selected Environmental Issues, coordinated by Jonathan L. Ramseur.

[8] See CRS Report R42537, Canadian Oil Sands: Life-Cycle Assessments of Greenhouse Gas Emissions, by Richard K. Lattanzio.

[9] See CRS Report R41398, The Dodd-Frank Wall Street Reform and Consumer Protection Act: Title VII, Derivatives, by Rena S. Miller and Kathleen Ann Ruane.

[10] See CRS Report R42460, The Strategic Petroleum Reserve: Authorization, Operation, and Drawdown Policy, by Anthony Andrews and Robert Pirog.

[11] See CRS Report R42074, U.S. Natural Gas Exports: New Opportunities, Uncertain Outcomes, by Michael Ratner et al.

[12] See CRS Report R41914, EPA's Regulation of Coal-Fired Power: Is a "Train Wreck" Coming?, by James E. McCarthy and Claudia Copeland.

[13] See CRS Report RL33558, Nuclear Energy Policy, by Mark Holt.

[14] See CRS Report R42152, Loan Guarantees for Clean Energy Technologies: Goals, Concerns, and Policy Options, by Phillip Brown.

[15] For a list of energy-related provisions that were extended as part of P.L. 112-240, see CRS Report R42894, An Overview of the Tax Provisions in the American Taxpayer Relief Act of 2012 , by Margot L. Crandall-Hollick.

[16] For more information, see CRS Report R43206, Energy Tax Policy: Issues in the 113th Congress, by Molly F. Sherlock; CRS Report R43124, Tax Provisions Expiring in 2013 ("Tax Extenders"), by Molly F. Sherlock; and CRS Report R42374, Oil and Natural Gas Industry Tax Issues in the FY2014 Budget Proposal, by Robert Pirog.

[17] For more information, see CRS Report R41668, Keystone XL Pipeline Project: Key Issues, by Paul W. Parfomak et al.

[18] For more information, see CRS Report R43138, Interstate Natural Gas Pipelines: Process and Timing of FERC Permit Application Review, by Paul W. Parfomak.

[19] See CRS Report R43120, President Obama's Climate Action Plan, coordinated by Jane A. Leggett.

[20] See CRS Report R43148, An Overview of Unconventional Oil and Natural Gas: Resources and Federal Actions, by Michael Ratner and Mary Tiemann.

[21] For details, see CRS Report R43259, S. 1392, Shaheen-Portman Bill: Energy Savings and Industrial Competitiveness Act of 2013, by Fred Sissine.

In: Energy Diversity for Economic Progress ISBN: 978-1-63321-577-1
Editor: Simone Williams

Chapter 4

AN OVERVIEW OF UNCONVENTIONAL OIL AND NATURAL GAS: RESOURCES AND FEDERAL ACTIONS[*]

Michael Ratner and Mary Tiemann

SUMMARY

The United States has seen a resurgence in petroleum production, mainly driven by technology improvements—hydraulic fracturing and directional drilling—developed for natural gas production from shale formations. Application of both of these technologies enabled natural gas to be economically produced from shale and other unconventional formations, and contributed to the United States becoming the world's largest natural gas producer in 2009. Use of these technologies has also contributed to the rise in U.S. oil production over the last few years. In 2009, annual oil production increased over 2008, the first annual rise since 1991, and has continued to increase each year since then. Between October 2007 and October 2013, U.S. monthly crude oil production rose by 2.7 million barrels per day, with about 92% of the increase coming from shale and related tight oil formations in Texas and North Dakota. Other tight oil plays are also being developed, and helped raise the prospect of energy independence, particularly for North America.

---

[*] This is an edited, reformatted and augmented version of a Congressional Research Service publication, No. R43148, dated January 23, 2014.

The rapid expansion of oil and gas extraction using hydraulic fracturing—both in rural and more densely populated areas—has raised concerns about its potential environmental and health impacts. These concerns have focused primarily on potential impacts to groundwater and surface water quality, public and private water supplies, and air quality.

States broadly regulate oil and gas exploration and production on non-federal lands. State laws and regulations governing unconventional oil and natural gas development have been evolving across the states in response to changes in production practices, largely in response to the use of high-volume hydraulic fracturing in combination with directional drilling. However, state regulations vary considerably, leading to calls for more federal regulation of unconventional oil and natural gas extraction activities.

Although several federal environmental laws can apply to certain activities related to oil and gas production, proposals to expand federal regulation in this area have been highly controversial. Some advocates of a larger federal role point to a wide range of differences among state regulatory regimes, and argue that a national framework is needed to ensure a consistent minimum level of protection for surface and groundwater resources, and air quality. Others argue against more federal involvement, and point to the long-established state oil and natural gas regulatory programs, regional differences in geology and water resources, and concern over regulatory redundancy.

The federal role in regulating oil and gas extraction activities—and hydraulic fracturing, in particular—has been the subject of considerable debate and legislative proposals for several years, but legislation has not been enacted. While congressional debate has continued, the Administration has pursued a number of regulatory initiatives related to unconventional oil and gas development under existing statutory authorities.

This report focuses on the growth in U.S. oil and natural gas production driven primarily by tight oil formations and shale gas formations. It also reviews selected federal environmental regulatory and research initiatives related to unconventional oil and gas extraction, including the Bureau of Land Management (BLM) proposed hydraulic fracturing rule and EPA actions.

INTRODUCTION: CHANGE IS AFOOT

In the past, the oil and natural gas industry considered resources locked in tight, impermeable formations like shale uneconomical to produce. Advances in directional well drilling and reservoir stimulation, however, have dramatically changed this perspective. It is production from these unconventional formations that has changed the U.S. energy posture and global energy markets.

U.S. oil and natural gas production is on the rise, primarily driven by resources from tight formations. The techniques developed to produce shale gas—directional drilling and hydraulic fracturing[1]—have migrated to the oil sector. The United States is the third-largest oil producer in the world, but also the fastest-growing producer. The United States surpassed Russia in 2009 as the world's largest natural gas producer. Production from tight formations is expected to make up a significant part of production of each commodity well into the future (see **Figure 1**).

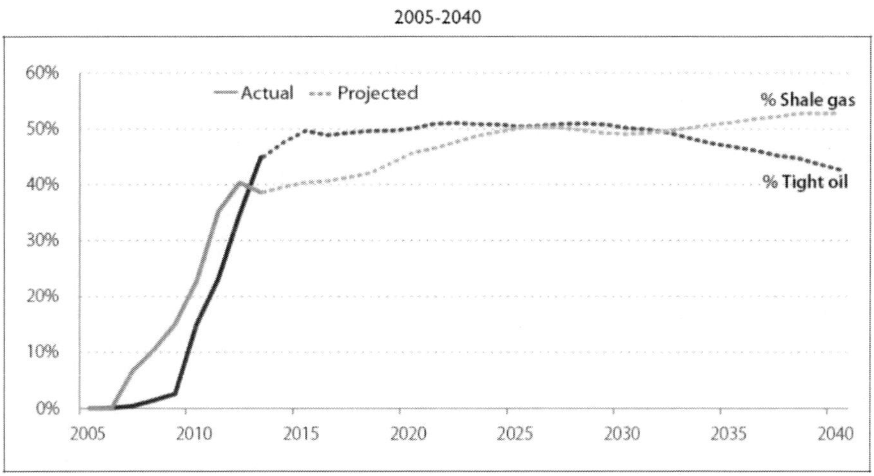

Source: U.S. Energy Information Administration, *Annual Energy Outlook 2014*, http://www.eia.gov/oiaf/aeo/ tablebrowser/ and other EIA data.

Note: Prior to 2007, the Energy Information Administration did not report tight oil and shale gas data.

Figure 1. Percentage of U.S. Oil and Natural Gas from Tight Oil and Shale Gas.

This report focuses on the growth in U.S. oil and natural gas production driven primarily by tight oil formations and shale gas formations. It does not address other types of unconventional production such as coalbed methane or tight gas, as their contributions to overall U.S. production have not changed as dramatically as shale gas.[2] There has been continued congressional interest through the 113th Congress related to unconventional natural gas and oil production. In May 2013, the Senate Energy and Natural Resources

Committee held three roundtable discussions on natural gas supply and use.[3] The House Energy and Commerce Committee's Subcommittee on Energy and Power held a hearing in June 2013 on U.S. energy abundance.[4]

GEOLOGY IS WHAT MAKES A RESOURCE UNCONVENTIONAL

Unconventional formations are fine-grained, organic-rich, sedimentary rocks—usually shales and similar rocks. The shales and rocks are both the source of and the reservoir for oil and natural gas, unlike conventional petroleum reservoirs. The Society of Petroleum Engineers describes "unconventional resources" as petroleum accumulations that are pervasive throughout a large area and that are not significantly affected by pressure exerted by water (hydrodynamic influences); they are also called "continuous-type deposits" or "tight formations." In contrast, conventional oil and natural gas occur in porous and permeable sandstone and carbonate reservoirs. Under pressure exerted by water, the hydrocarbons migrated upward from organic sources until an impermeable cap-rock (such as shale) trapped it in the reservoir rock. Although the unconventional formations may be as porous as other sedimentary reservoir rocks, their extremely small pore sizes and lack of permeability make them relatively resistant to hydrocarbon flow. The lack of permeability means that the oil and gas typically remain in the source rock unless natural or artificial fractures occur.

PRICE DRIVES INDUSTRIAL INNOVATION

Historically, natural gas prices in the United States have been volatile. From 1995 to 1999 the spot price of natural gas averaged $2.23 per million British thermal units (MBtu), but increased to an average price of $4.68 per MBtu, in nominal dollars, during the 2000-to-2004 period, an almost 110% rise. Prices hit a peak in December 2005 at $15.38 per MBtu, but remained relatively high through July 2008, as can be seen in **Figure 2**. Along with the rise in prices, U.S. net imports of natural gas also rose, increasing 32% between 1995 and 2000 and 41% between 1995 and 2007.

2002-2013

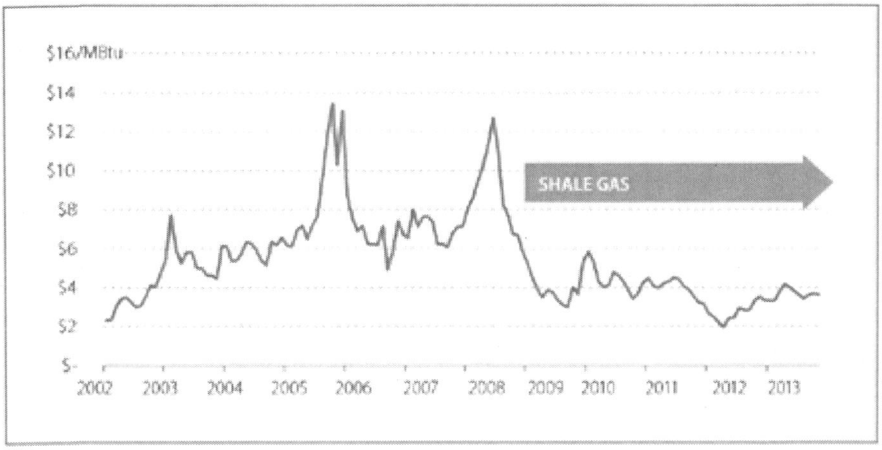

Source: U.S. Energy Information Administration.

Note: Units = nominal dollars per million British thermal units (MBtu). Data for 2013 are through November.

Figure 2. Daily U.S. Natural.

As U.S. prices and imports continued to trend up, industry undertook two competing solutions to meet the need for more natural gas—increased liquefied natural gas (LNG) imports and development of techniques to produce shale gas. The LNG import facilities were much higher-profile and were cited extensively in industry and popular press. Approximately 50 import projects were proposed, and eight were eventually constructed during the mid- to late 2000s, along with the recommissioning of older facilities.

Although horizontal drilling and hydraulic fracturing have been industry techniques for some time, their application to shale gas formations is relatively new. Advances in directional drilling, particularly steerable down-hole motors, allowed drilling operators to better keep the well bore in the hydrocarbon-bearing shale formations. Well stimulation was also required, and improvements in hydraulic fracturing techniques, particularly multistage hydraulic fracturing and the ability to better control the fractures, contributed to making shale gas production a profitable venture.

In 2007, the Energy Information Administration (EIA) first recorded shale gas production, when it accounted for just 7% of U.S. natural gas production. In 2013, shale gas production accounted for almost 40% of U.S. production, while almost all the LNG import terminals are idle and many have applied to become export terminals.[5]

Technologies Stimulate Shale Gas Production First

The application of advances in directional drilling and hydraulic fracturing were first applied to shale gas formations, particularly as natural gas prices increased in the mid-2000s. Methane molecules and those of natural gas liquids (NGLs) are smaller than crude oil molecules and therefore tend to be more responsive to hydraulic fracturing. The success of shale gas development has driven U.S. natural gas production to increase almost every month on a year-onyear basis (see **Figure 3**) from 2007 through 2013. The rise in shale gas development has also resulted in natural gas prices declining, as shown in **Figure 2**.

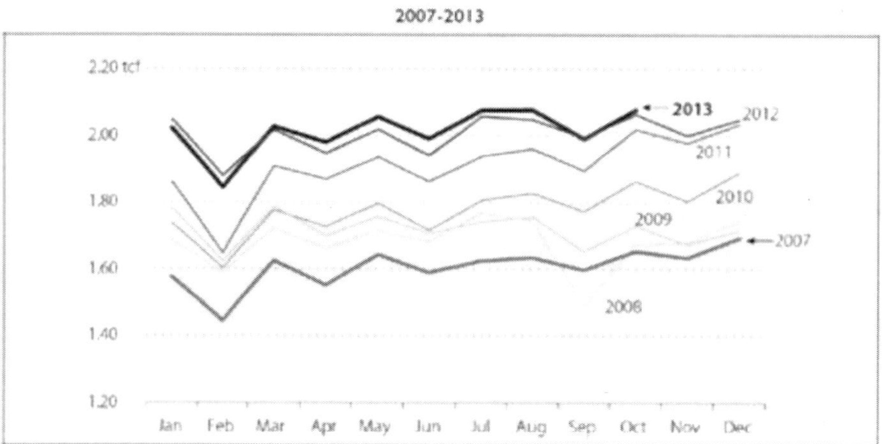

Source: U.S. Energy Information Administration. Note: Units = trillion cubic feet (tcf).

Figure 3. Monthly U.S. Natural Gas Production.

The decline in prices and production in the latter half of 2008 was mainly the result of the economic downturn. However, as the economy picked up in 2009, natural gas resumed its upward production trajectory while prices stayed low. Overall U.S. natural gas production grew, as did the contribution from shale. The continued increase in production can be attributed, in part, to industry improvements in extracting more of the natural gas from the shale formations. Continued progress in hydraulic fracturing and directional drilling techniques has enabled companies to drive down production costs while increasing output.

Natural Gas Liquids: A Production Driver

Natural gas liquids (NGLs) have taken on a new prominence as shale gas production has increased and prices have fallen. As natural gas prices have stayed low, company interests have shifted away from dry natural gas production to more liquids-based production. NGL is a general term for all liquid products separated from natural gas at a gas processing plant, and includes ethane, propane, butane, and pentanes. When NGLs are present with methane, which is the primary component of natural gas, the natural gas is referred to as either "hot" or "wet" gas. Once the NGLs are removed from the methane, the natural gas is referred to as "dry" gas, which is what most consumers use.

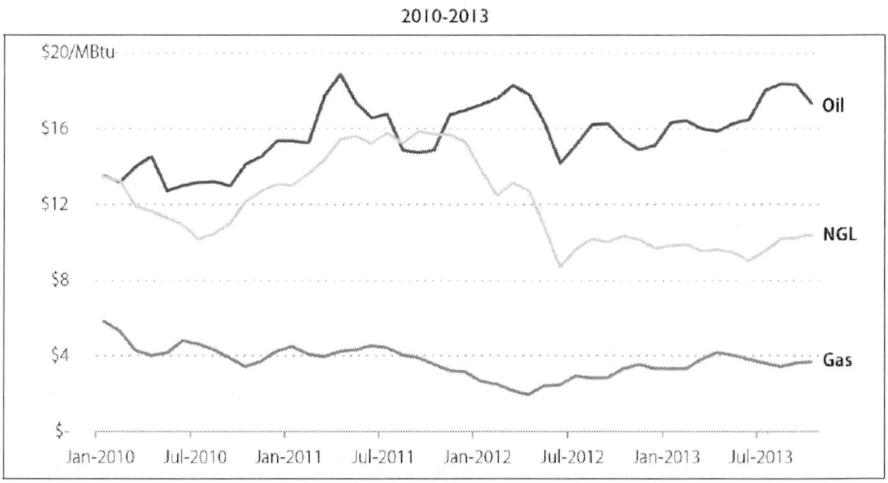

Source: U.S. Energy Information Administration.

Notes: According to EIA, the NGL composite price is derived from daily Bloomberg spot price data for natural gas liquids at Mont Belvieu, TX, weighted by gas processing plant production volumes of each product as reported on Form EIA-816, "Monthly Natural Gas Liquids Report." The mix of NGLs will vary by source, and the price will vary by the actual market for the product. The natural gas price is at Henry Hub, and the oil price is West Texas Intermediate (WTI). Units = nominal dollars per million British thermal units (MBtu).

Figure 4. Natural Gas, Oil, and NGL Prices.

Each NGL has its own market and its own value. As the price for dry gas has dropped because of the increase in supply and other reasons, such as the warm winter of 2011, the natural gas industry has turned its attention to producing in areas with more wet gas in order to bolster the value it receives (see **Figure 4**). Some companies have shifted their production portfolios to tight oil formations, such as the Bakken in North Dakota and Montana, to capitalize on the experience they gained in shale gas development. Historically, the individual NGL products have been priced against oil, except for ethane. As oil prices have remained higher since 2008 relative to natural gas, they have driven an increase of wet gas production. Because of its low price, dry gas is often treated as a "by-product" of wet gas and oil production, despite its low price.

Increased Tight Oil Production Raises Independence Possibility

The prospect of U.S. energy independence is grounded in the production growth from tight oil formations such as the Bakken Formation in North Dakota and Montana, and the Eagle Ford Formation in Texas.[6] Relative to other fuels, the United States is more dependent upon imports for its oil requirements, still accounting for almost 40% of consumption.[7] Canada is the largest supplier of U.S. oil imports, which is why energy independence is usually mentioned as North American energy independence.[8] The United States added a total of more than 800,000 barrels per day (b/d) of oil production between October 2012 and October 2013 (see **Figure 5**). U.S. oil production has reached levels not seen in more than a decade, but is almost 2.5 million b/d short of the highs in the 1970s. Since June 2005, when crude oil imports reached a peak, they have dropped almost 3.3 million b/d, or 23%, through October 2013.[9] Also since 2005, U.S. consumption of crude oil and petroleum products has been trending downward, contributing to the decrease in imports.

The continued shift of industry resources toward oil-rich production has prompted forecasts of continued growth. Domestic crude oil production is projected to rise through the end of the decade. The tremendous increases are primarily due to dramatic increases in production from the previously mentioned Bakken Formation in North Dakota and the Eagle Ford play in Texas, both tight oil formations.[10]

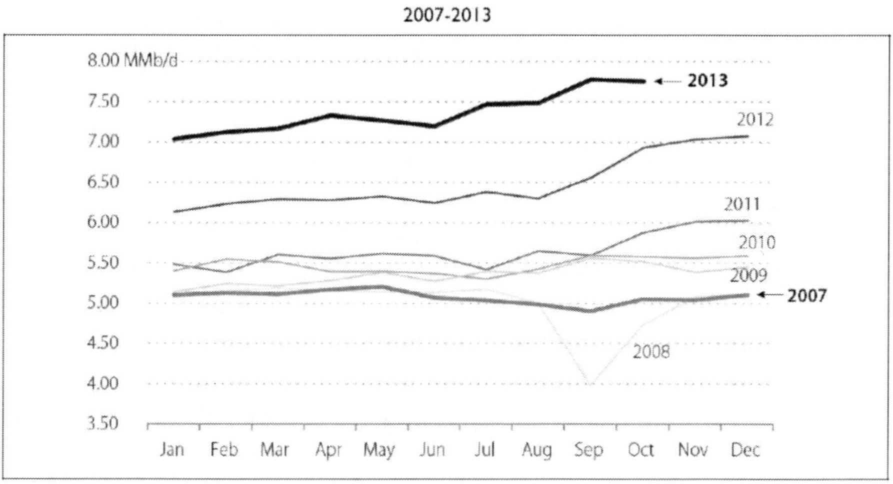

Source: U.S. Energy Information Administration.
Note: Units = million barrels per day (MMb/d).

Figure 5. Monthly U.S. Oil Production.

ENVIRONMENTAL CONCERNS AND RESPONSES

As with other energy sources or fuel production, the development of unconventional oil and gas resources can pose environmental risks, many of which potentially may be mitigated with appropriate safeguards and existing technology. The recent large-scale increase in unconventional oil and gas production may result in both negative and positive environmental impacts, comparatively speaking. For example, increased unconventional oil and gas production activity has in some cases placed a strain on water resources, and on wastewater treatment plants that were not designed to remove chemicals, salts, and other contaminants from hydraulic fracturing flowback and produced water. On the other hand, natural gas is seen by many as a "bridge" fuel that can provide more energy per unit of greenhouse gas produced than some alternatives (e.g., coal), and has only recently been produced in sufficient quantity and at low enough prices to provide a viable alternative fuel that is widely regarded as relatively cleaner-burning.

Nonetheless, the rapid expansion of oil and natural gas extraction using high-volume hydraulic fracturing—both in rural and more densely populated areas—has generated controversy due to its potential scale and impacts on land and water resources, air quality, communities, and landowners.[11]

Water quality issues have received the most attention, and of these, the potential risks associated with well stimulation by hydraulic fracturing have been at the forefront. Complaints of contaminated well water have emerged in various areas where unconventional oil and gas development is occurring,[12] although regulators have not reported a direct connection between hydraulic fracturing of shale formations at depth and groundwater contamination. In shale formations, the vertical distance separating the target zone from usable aquifers generally is much greater than the length of the fractures induced during hydraulic fracturing. Thousands of feet of rock layers typically overlay the produced portion of shale, and these layers serve as barriers to flow. In these circumstances, geologists and state regulators generally view as remote the possibility of creating a fracture that could reach a potable aquifer. If the shallow portions of shale formations were developed, then the thickness of the overlying rocks would be less and the distance from the shale to potable aquifers would be shorter, posing more of a risk to groundwater. In contrast to shale, coalbed methane (CBM) basins often qualify as underground sources of drinking water. Injection of fracturing fluids directly into or adjacent to such formations would be more likely to present a risk of contamination, and this is where initial regulatory attention and study was focused.[13]

State regulators have expressed more concern about the groundwater contamination risks associated with developing a natural gas or oil well (drilling through an overlying aquifer and casing, cementing, and completing the well), as opposed to hydraulic fracturing per se. The challenges of sealing off the groundwater and isolating it from possible contamination are common to the development of any oil or gas well, and are not unique to hydraulic fracturing.

Identifying the source or cause of groundwater contamination can be difficult for various reasons, including the complexity of hydrogeologic processes and investigations, a lack of baseline testing of nearby water wells prior to drilling and fracturing, and the confidential business information status traditionally provided for fracturing compounds. In cases that have been investigated, regulators generally have determined that groundwater contamination was caused by failure of well-bore casing and cementing, well operation problems, or surface activities, rather than the hydraulic fracturing process.[14]

The debate over the groundwater contamination risks associated with hydraulic fracturing operations has been fueled in part by the lack of scientific studies to assess more thoroughly the current practices and related complaints and uncertainties. To help address this issue, Congress has directed the

Environmental Protection Agency (EPA) to conduct a study on the relationship between hydraulic fracturing and drinking water.[15] The "hydraulic fracturing" debate also has been complicated by terminology. Many who express concern over the potential environmental impacts associated with hydraulic fracturing do not differentiate the well stimulation process of "fracing" or "fracking" from the full range of activities associated with unconventional oil and gas exploration and production.[16]

The management of the large volumes of wastewater produced during natural gas production (including flowback from hydraulic fracturing operations and water produced from source formations) has emerged as a significant water quality issue. In some areas, such as portions of the Marcellus Shale region,[17] capacity is limited for wastewater disposal using underground injection wells (historically, the most common produced-water disposal practice in oil and natural gas fields), and surface discharge of wastewater is an increasingly restricted option. Additionally, the injection of large volumes of wastewater into disposal wells has been associated with some instances of induced seismicity.[18]

Other water quality concerns—associated with both conventional and unconventional oil and natural gas extraction—include the risks of contaminating ground and surface water from surface spills, migration of methane gas and contaminants into residential water wells from faulty well construction, and siltation of streams from drilling and pad construction activities.[19] Because of the large, but short-term, volumes of water needed for the hydraulic fracturing operations used to extract shale gas and tight oil, water consumption issues have emerged as well. Water use issues include the impacts that large water withdrawals might have on groundwater resources, streams and aquatic life (particularly during low-flow periods), and other competing uses (e.g., municipal or agricultural uses).

Air pollution associated with unconventional oil and natural gas production has also raised public health concerns and has drawn regulatory scrutiny. Air pollutants can be released during various stages of oil and natural gas production, not just hydraulic fracturing. Emission sources include pad, road, and pipeline construction; well drilling and completion, and flowback activities; and natural gas processing, storage, and transmission equipment. Key pollutants include methane (the main component of natural gas and a potent greenhouse gas), volatile organic compounds (VOCs), nitrogen oxides, sulfur dioxide, particulate matter, and various hazardous air pollutants.[20] According to EPA, the oil and gas industry is a significant source of VOCs, which react with nitrogen oxides to form ozone (smog). EPA has identified hydraulically fractured gas wells during flowback as an additional source of VOC emissions in the natural gas industry.[21]

In addition to hydraulically fractured gas wells, releases of methane and other pollutants can occur where natural gas is produced in association with oil, and natural gas gathering pipelines and other infrastructure are lacking. In such cases, the natural gas generally must be flared or vented. Flaring reduces VOC emissions compared to venting, but like venting, it contributes to greenhouse gas emissions without producing an economic value or displacing other fuel consumption.[22] Natural gas flaring has become an issue with the rapid and intense development of tight oil from the Bakken Formation in North Dakota, which has significant amounts of associated gas.[23] Other areas that have experienced large increases in tight oil production also have had increases in the amount of natural gas being flared.

State Regulation of Oil and Gas Development

Oil and natural gas development is occurring in at least 32 states.[24] Shale gas, tight oil, or other unconventional resources are found in many of these states; primarily on non-federal lands (see **Figure 6**). States are the principal regulators of oil and gas exploration and production activities on state and private lands.[25] Additionally, some states require operators on federal public lands within state boundaries to comply with the state's oil and gas rules.[26]

Hydraulic fracturing has been used for decades to stimulate increased production from existing oil or gas wells. This technique, along with other well stimulation techniques, has been regulated to varying degrees through state oil and gas codes. The detail and scope of applicable regulations vary across the states, and some states have regulated "well stimulation" broadly without addressing hydraulic "fracturing" explicitly.[27] State regulators have noted that hydraulic fracturing operations are regulated through provisions that address various production activities, including requirements regarding well construction (e.g., casing and cementing), well stimulation (e.g., hydraulic fracturing), and well operation (e.g., pressure testing and blowout prevention). Nonetheless, state groundwater protection officials also have reported that development of shale gas and tight oil using high-volume hydraulic fracturing, in combination with directional drilling, has posed new challenges for the management and protection of water resources.[28]

Consequently, many of the major producing states have revised or are in the process of revising their oil and gas laws and regulations to respond to these advances in oil and natural gas production technologies and related changes in the industry.[29]

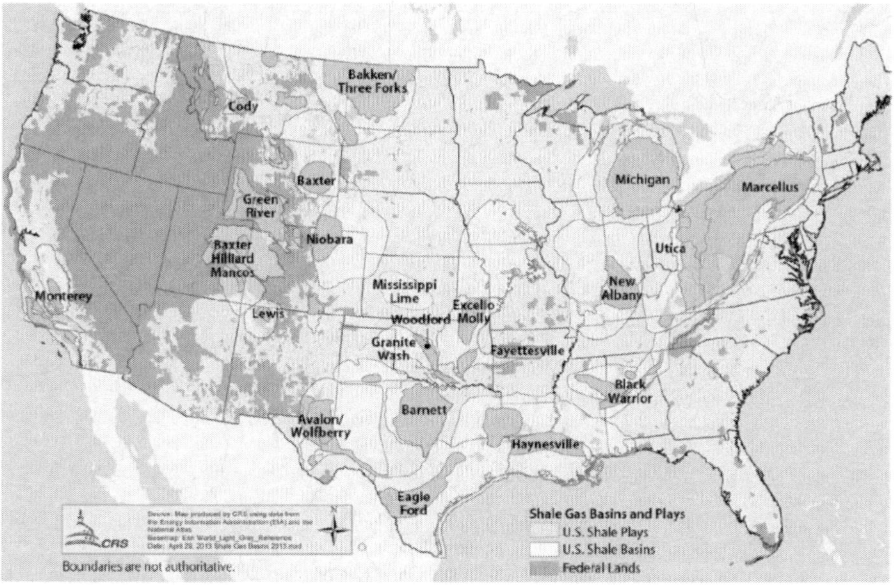

Source: CRS, compiled from U.S. Energy Information Administration sources.

Notes: No information had been reported on active shale plays in Alaska at the time of this report. Hawaii's volcanic origin does not support the geologic process leading to the deposition of shale.

Figure 6. Unconventional Shale Plays in the Lower 48 States. (with federal lands shown).

When revising measures, states have added provisions to address hydraulic fracturing specifically, such as requirements for disclosure of chemicals used in hydraulic fracturing.[30] Other common revisions include stricter requirements for well construction and operation (e.g., cementing, casing, and pressure testing) and wastewater storage and disposal.[31] New York State has imposed a de facto moratorium on high-volume hydraulic fracturing pending completion of environmental and public health reviews and development of new rules. Similarly, Maryland regulators, pursuant to executive order, are studying the risks associated with deep drilling and hydraulic fracturing to identify new safeguards that may be needed in permits. North Carolina has enacted legislation that prohibits the issuance of permits for oil and gas development using hydraulic fracturing and horizontal drilling until new regulations and standards are in place and the legislature takes affirmative action to allow permits to be issued.[32]

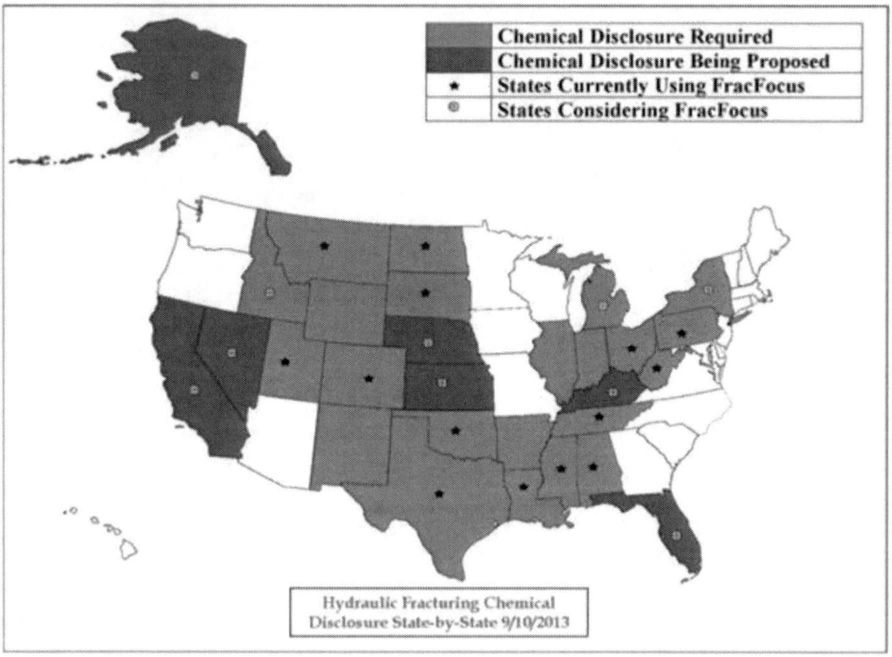

Source: Ground Water Protection Council, *Groundwater Communique*, September 2013.

Notes: FracFocus was established in 2011 by the Ground Water Protection Council and the Interstate Oil and Gas Compact Commission (IOGCC). FracFocus is a public registry where oil and gas companies may voluntarily identify chemicals used in hydraulic fracturing operations at specific wells. Many states allow or require operators to meet state disclosure requirements by posting information on the FracFocus website (http://www.fracfocus.org).

California legislation, enacted in September 2013, allows disclosure through FracFocus until a state website becomes operational. Also, the proposed Bureau of Land Management hydraulic fracturing rule would allow companies to meet chemical disclosure requirements using the FracFocus website.

Figure 7. Hydraulic Fracturing Chemical Disclosure by State.

The National Conference of State Legislatures (NCSL) reported that "state legislatures are actively working to address public health and environmental concerns, while also taking advantage of the economic potential offered by shale gas development."[33] During the 2011-2012 legislative session, more than

170 bills were introduced in 29 states, and 14 of the states enacted legislation related to natural gas development.[34] The proposals covered a broad range of issues, and included measures on (1) water resources protection (including casing, well spacing, setbacks, water withdrawal, flowback, waste management requirements); (2) disclosure of hydraulic fracturing fluids; (3) severance taxes; (4) hydraulic fracturing suspensions, moratoria, or studies to investigate impacts; and (5) resolutions addressing hydraulic fracturing.[35] Regarding disclosure of chemicals used in hydraulic fracturing fluids, at least 35 bills were introduced in 14 states, and legislation was enacted in three states (Indiana, Louisiana, and Pennsylvania). According to the Ground Water Protection Council, by September 10, 2013, at least 22 states had adopted chemical disclosure requirements, and public disclosure was required in 13 states, while other states were considering such requirements (see **Figure 7**).[36] In late September 2013, California enacted legislation broadly regulating hydraulic fracturing and other well stimulation processes. Among other provisions, the California law requires public disclosure of chemicals, baseline water testing, and groundwater monitoring, and directs the state to conduct a comprehensive study on the environmental impacts associated with well stimulation and hydraulic fracturing.

Debate over the Federal Role

While states continue to adopt and implement varying frameworks for oversight and regulation of unconventional gas and oil development, numerous citizen and environmental groups and Members of Congress have pressed for greater environmental oversight of shale energy development at the federal level. Some advocates of a larger federal role point to a wide range of differences in substance, scope, and enforcement among state regulatory regimes, and assert that a national framework is needed to ensure a consistent baseline level of environmental and human health protection and transparency.[37] Such advocates further argue that greater regulatory uniformity would reduce risks and uncertainties to both the industry and the public.[38] Others argue against greater federal involvement, and point to established state oil and gas programs and regulatory structures (which include a range of structures involving commissions, boards, or divisions within natural resource agencies working to varying degrees with, or within, state environmental agencies). In this view, experience lies with the states, and in addition to the relative nimbleness of states to review and revise laws and rules, the states are better able to consider regional differences in geology, topography, climate, and water resources.

In the 113th Congress, as in recent Congresses, the federal role in regulating oil and gas production generally, and hydraulic fracturing specifically, has been the subject of hearings, seminars, and legislation.[39] A number of bills have been proposed to broaden the federal role, while others have proposed to further limit federal involvement in regulating oil and gas development. Such proposals have been contentious, and Congress has not enacted such legislation since amending the Safe Drinking Water Act (SDWA) in the Energy Policy Act (EPAct) of 2005 (P.L. 109-58) to explicitly exclude from the SDWA definition of underground injection the injection of fluids (other than diesel fuels) related to hydraulic fracturing operations.[40]

Selected Federal Responses to Unconventional Resource Extraction

Provisions of several federal environmental laws and related regulations currently apply to certain activities associated with oil and natural gas production. The Clean Water Act (CWA), for example, prohibits the discharge of pollutants from point sources into surface waters without a permit,[41] and the Safe Drinking Water Act (SDWA) requires an Underground Injection Control (UIC) permit for wastewater disposal through deep well injection.[42] Additionally, a SDWA UIC permit is required for the underground injection of fluids or propping agents pursuant to hydraulic fracturing if the injected fracturing fluids contain diesel fuels.[43] In 2012, EPA promulgated regulations under the authority of the Clean Air Act that require reductions in emissions related to oil and natural gas production, including emissions of volatile organic compounds (VOCs) from hydraulically fractured natural gas wells.[44]

While congressional debate has continued on legislative proposals, the Administration has been pursuing additional initiatives to regulate or otherwise manage activities related to unconventional oil and natural gas production, and hydraulic fracturing specifically. EPA has been most active, and is considering actions under several pollution control statutes. Among these efforts, EPA is working to (1) establish pretreatment standards to control discharges of wastewater from shale gas extraction to publicly owned wastewater treatment plants; (2) revise water quality criteria to protect aquatic life from discharges of brine produced during oil and gas extraction to surface waters; (3) subject hydraulic fracturing chemicals to toxic substance reporting requirements;[45] and (4) finalize permitting guidance for the use of diesel in hydraulic fracturing operations. The Appendix of this report provides a brief overview of selected federal environmental research and regulatory activities related to the production of tight oil and gas resources. Several of these initiatives are reviewed below.

EPA Study on Hydraulic Fracturing and Drinking Water

In 2009, the 111th Congress urged EPA to conduct a study on the relationship between hydraulic fracturing and drinking water to gain a better understanding of potential contamination risks.[46] In 2011, EPA published a final study plan that identified research projects that would address the full life cycle of water in hydraulic fracturing, from water acquisition to chemical mixing and injection through wastewater treatment and/or disposal. The study is intended to (1) examine conditions that may be associated with potential contamination of drinking water sources, and (2) identify factors that may lead to human exposure and risks.[47] As part of the study, EPA is investigating five reported incidents of drinking water contamination in areas where hydraulic fracturing has occurred. The purpose of the retrospective case studies is to determine the potential relationship between reported impacts and hydraulic fracturing activities.[48]

In December 2012, EPA released a status report presenting the agency's efforts through FY2012 on 18 research projects being conducted for the study.[49] No data or findings were included. EPA plans to issue individual reports and papers during 2013 and 2014, and to synthesize the results from the research projects in a draft "report of results" by the end of 2014. EPA has designated the report of results as a "highly influential scientific assessment" (HISA),[50] which will undergo peer review by EPA's Science Advisory Board.[51] In June 2013, the agency announced that the final report will not be completed before 2016.

Multiagency Collaboration on Unconventional Oil and Gas Research

In March 2011, the White House issued a broad *Blueprint for a Secure Energy Future*, which identifies the need to "expand safe and responsible domestic oil and gas development and production." Additionally, the President directed the Secretary of the Department of Energy (DOE) to identify steps that could be taken to improve the safety and environmental performance of shale gas production, and to develop consensus recommendations on practices to ensure the protection of public health and the environment.[52]

In response, the Secretary of Energy's Advisory Board (SEAB) convened the Shale Gas Production Subcommittee to evaluate hydraulic fracturing issues and make recommendations to mitigate possible impacts of shale gas development. The final report included recommendations for the states, federal government, and industry. The subcommittee recommended, among other actions, that companies and regulators—to the extent that such actions had not been undertaken— adopt further measures to protect water quality and to manage water use and wastewater disposal, publicly report the composition of water and flow throughout the fracturing and cleanup process, disclose fracturing fluid composition, and adopt best practices for well development and construction (especially casing, cementing, and pressure management).[53]

In 2012, the President issued Executive Order (E.O.) 13605, *Supporting Safe and Responsible Development of Unconventional Domestic Natural Gas Resources*, to coordinate the efforts of federal agencies overseeing the development of unconventional domestic natural gas resources and associated infrastructure. The order states that "Because efforts to promote safe, responsible, and efficient development of unconventional domestic natural gas resources are underway at a number of executive departments and agencies, close interagency coordination is important for effective implementation of these programs and activities."[54]

E.O. 13605 established an interagency working group to coordinate agency activities and to engage in long-term planning and ensure coordination on research, resource assessment, and infrastructure development. In April 2012, the lead agencies—DOE, EPA, and the Department of the Interior (DOI/U.S. Geological Survey)—signed a Memorandum of Agreement to develop a multiagency research plan "to address the highest priority research questions associated with safely and prudently developing unconventional shale gas and tight oil reserves."[55]

BLM Proposed Rule on Hydraulic Fracturing

While states have predominant regulatory authority for oil and gas development on state and private lands, the federal government is responsible for managing oil and gas resources on federal lands. However, some states require oil and gas operators on federal lands within their state to comply with state rules, and consequently, the debate over the federal role in regulating unconventional oil and gas production has extended to activities on federal lands.

The Bureau of Land Management (BLM), within the Department of the Interior, is the federal agency responsible for overseeing oil, natural gas, and coal leasing and production on federal and Indian lands, including split estate where the federal government owns the subsurface mineral estate.[56] BLM is tasked with leasing subsurface mineral rights not only on BLM-administered land, but also for lands managed by other federal agencies, including the U.S. Forest Service.[57] BLM oversees roughly 700 million subsurface acres of federal mineral estate and 56 million subsurface acres of Indian mineral estate nationwide. BLM estimates that approximately 3,400 wells have been drilled annually in recent years on federal and Indian lands, and that hydraulic fracturing is used to stimulate roughly 90% of these wells.[58]

In May 2012, BLM proposed revisions to its oil and natural gas development rules in response to the increased use of hydraulic fracturing on federal and Indian lands.[59] The proposed rule broadly addressed "well stimulation, including hydraulic fracturing," and would revise BLM oil and gas production regulations that were promulgated in 1982 and last revised in 1988.[60] In the 2012 *Federal Register* notice, BLM noted that the rule would modernize its management of well stimulation activities, and stated that the "rule is necessary to provide useful information to the public and to assure that hydraulic fracturing is conducted in a way that adequately protects the environment." [61] The preamble further noted that the proposed changes were partly in response to recommendations made by the aforementioned SEAB Shale Gas Subcommittee.

BLM received more than 177,000 comments on the proposed rule, and in May 2013, BLM published a Supplemental Notice of Proposed Rulemaking (SNPR) and Request for Comment. BLM has requested comments on the multiple changes in the proposed rule, and provided 30 days for public comment. (The comment period was extended for 60 days, to August 23, 2013.)[62]

Changes notwithstanding, the 2012 proposed rule and the 2013 SNPR share overarching features that reflect recommendations of the SEAB subcommittee report. Both proposals would (1) add reporting and management requirements for water and other fluids used and produced in hydraulic fracturing operations, with emphasis on managing fluids that flow back to the surface, (2) require public disclosure of hydraulic fracturing chemicals, and (3) tighten well construction and operation requirements to help ensure that wellbore integrity is maintained throughout the hydraulic fracturing process.

Among the changes to the 2012 proposed rule, the BLM 2013 Supplemental Notice would

- narrow the scope of the rule to apply only to hydraulic fracturing and refracturing (the 2012 proposed rule would have applied to "well stimulation" activities broadly);[63]
- provide opportunities for individual states or tribes to work with BLM to craft variances for specific regulatory provisions that would allow compliance with state or tribal requirements to be accepted as compliance with the BLM rule (if the variance would meet or exceed the effectiveness of the rule provision it would replace);[64]
- allow operators to report hydraulic fracturing chemical information to BLM either directly or through the FracFocus website or other specified database,[65] and provide more detailed guidance on procedures for handling trade secret claims;[66]
- clarify that mechanical integrity testing would be required for all fracturing and refracturing operations;[67]
- require that all fracturing operations isolate all usable water formations to protect them from contamination, and allow operators to use an expanded set of cement evaluation tools to help ensure that usable water zones have been isolated and protected;[68] and
- allow an advanced Notice of Intent to be submitted for a single well, or group of wells with the same geological characteristics within a field where hydraulic fracturing operations are likely to be successful using the same design.[69]

BLM also requested comment on whether to require hydraulic fracturing wastewater to be stored in tanks only, rather than in lined pits or tanks as proposed in 2012.

Coast Guard Regulation of Barge Shipments of Shale Gas Wastewater

The disposal of the large volumes of wastewater produced during shale gas extraction has posed challenges for companies, state regulators, and communities—particularly in the Marcellus Shale region. On-site disposal options are limited, and trucking wastewater to distant injection wells is costly. In 2012, the Coast Guard received two requests for approval for the bulk shipment of wastewater resulting from shale gas extraction in the Marcellus Shale to storage or treatment centers and final disposal sites in Ohio, Texas, and Louisiana.

The Coast Guard regulates the shipment of hazardous materials on the nation's rivers, and classifies cargoes for bulk shipment.[70] For a cargo that has not been classified in the regulations or under prior policy, the ship owner must request Coast Guard approval prior to shipping the cargo.[71] The Coast Guard has identified concerns with shipment of shale gas wastewater in barges. A key Coast Guard concern with the wastewater is "its potential for contamination with radioactive isotopes such as radium-226 and -228. Radium is of particular concern because it is chemically similar to calcium and so will easily form surface residues and may lead to radioactive surface contamination of the barges."[72] Consequently, the Coast Guard currently does not allow barge shipment of shale gas extraction wastewater (SGEWW), and is developing a draft policy to allow SGEWW to be transported for disposal. In March, the Coast Guard submitted for review to the Office of Management and Budget (OMB) a draft document, "Carriage of Conditionally Permitted Shale Gas Extraction Waste Water in Bulk."

In October 2013, the Coast Guard published a notice of availability of a proposed "policy letter" concerning barge shipments of SGEWW and requested public comment. After reviewing comments, the Coast Guard plans to issue a final policy letter that specifies conditions and information requirements that barge owners would be required to meet to receive approval to transport shale gas wastewater in bulk on inland waterways.[73]

LEGISLATION IN THE 113TH CONGRESS

Contrasting bills have been offered in the 113th Congress addressing unconventional oil and gas development, and hydraulic fracturing specifically. Several bills would expand federal regulation of hydraulic fracturing activities, while others would limit federal involvement.[74] House-passed H.R. 2728 would amend the Mineral Leasing Act[75] to prohibit the Department of the Interior from enforcing any federal regulation, guidance, or permit requirement regarding hydraulic fracturing relating to oil, gas, or geothermal production activities on or under any land in any state that has regulations, guidance, or permit requirements for hydraulic fracturing. Although this language is broadly applicable to any federal regulation, guidance, and permit requirements "regarding hydraulic fracturing," the prohibition on enforcement applies only to the Department of the Interior, and therefore would presumably impact only hydraulic fracturing operations on lands managed by that agency. The bill also would require the Department of the Interior to defer to state regulations, permitting, and guidance for all activities related to hydraulic fracturing relating to oil, gas, or geothermal production activities on federal land regardless of whether those rules were duplicative, more or less restrictive, or did not meet federal guidelines. As reported, the bill would further prohibit the department from enforcing hydraulic fracturing regulations on Trust lands, except with express tribal consent. On November 12, 2013, the House Committee on Natural Resources reported H.R. 2728, amended, and the House passed the bill, amended, on November 20. The same day, S. 1743, a companion bill to H.R. 2728, as introduced, was offered in the Senate. H.R. 2728 was placed on the Senate Legislative Calendar on December 9, 2013.

Relatedly, the Fracturing Regulations are Effective in State Hands (FRESH) Act, H.R. 2513 and S. 1234, would establish that a state has sole authority to regulate hydraulic fracturing operations on lands within the boundaries of the state. The legislation further specifies that hydraulic fracturing on federal public lands shall be subject to the law of the state in which the land is located. H.R. 1548 (H.Rept. 113-263) would prohibit the BLM hydraulic fracturing rule from having any effect on land held in trust or restricted status for Indians, except with the express consent of its Indian beneficiaries.

Similarly, S. 1482, the Empower States Act of 2013 generally would prohibit the Secretary of the Interior from issuing regulations or guidelines regarding oil and gas production on federal land in a state if the state has otherwise met the requirements under applicable federal law. Among other provisions, the bill also would (1) amend the Safe Drinking Water Act to require federal agencies, before issuing any oil and gas regulation or guideline, to seek comment and consult with each affected state agency and Indian tribe, and (2) require any future rule requiring disclosure of hydraulic fracturing chemicals to refer to the FracFocus database.

In contrast to the above bills, several others propose to expand federal regulation of hydraulic fracturing. In the first session, the Fracturing Responsibility and Awareness of Chemicals Act (FRAC) of 2013 was introduced in the House (H.R. 1921) and the Senate (S. 1135). The bills would amend the Safe Drinking Water Act to (1) require disclosure of the chemicals used in the fracturing process, and (2) repeal the hydraulic fracturing exemption established in EPAct 2005 and amend the term "underground injection" to include the injection of fluids used in hydraulic fracturing operations, thus authorizing EPA to regulate this process under the SDWA. The Climate Protection Act of 2013, S. 332, Section 301, contains similar chemical disclosure provisions.

Additionally, S. 332 would repeal SDWA Section 1425, which provides states with an alternative to meeting the specific requirements contained in EPA UIC regulations promulgated under Section 1421 by allowing states to demonstrate to EPA that their existing programs for oil and gas injection wells are effective in preventing endangerment of underground sources of drinking water.[76] S. 332, Section 302, would require EPA to report to Congress on fugitive methane emissions resulting from natural gas infrastructure.

Legislation also has been introduced to require baseline and follow-up testing of potable groundwater supplies in the vicinity of hydraulic fracturing operations. H.R. 2983, the Safe Hydration is an American Right in Energy Development Act of 2013, would amend the SDWA to prohibit hydraulic fracturing unless the person proposing to conduct the fracturing operations agreed to testing and reporting requirements regarding underground sources of drinking water.

The legislation would require testing prior to the start of injection operations, and at prescribed intervals during and after hydraulic fracturing operations. Testing would be required for any contaminant or substance EPA determined would indicate damage associated with hydraulic fracturing operations. Additionally, H.R. 2983 would require EPA to post on its website all test results, searchable by zip code.

H.R. 2850 (H.Rept. 113-252), the EPA Hydraulic Fracturing Study Improvement Act, would require EPA to follow certain procedures governing peer review and data presentation in conducting its study on the relationship between hydraulic fracturing and drinking water. As reported, the bill would require EPA to release the final report by September 30, 2016. H.R. 2850 was placed on the Union Calendar on October 23, 2013.

Conclusion: Above- and Below-Ground Issues a Concern

The prospect that by the end of the decade the United States could become a significant exporter of natural gas and the world's leading oil producer is a phenomenal change of circumstances from just a few years ago. The technological advances that drove the changes in the United States have also reversed the global perspective of dwindling oil and natural gas resources, and increased the concern among many about greenhouse gas emissions. Other countries seek to emulate the U.S. success, but have yet to do so. The U.S. oil and gas situation continues to be extremely dynamic, and many questions remain about how the United States will develop its resources.

Many observers, including U.S. government officials, have only recently recognized the tremendous resource size and the benefits that will accrue from developing the resources, as well as the potential risks that may be associated with this development.

Even though shale gas development is still considered very new and tight oil production is even newer, the industry has continued to improve its efficiency in extracting the resources, particularly of natural gas. As more industry resources are shifted to tight oil plays, the natural gas sector has had to produce more with less. Some in industry point out that at the beginning of shale gas development about 5% of the resource was able to be extracted; now it is closer to 20%. By comparison, the extraction rate from conventional gas is between 30% and 60% of the resource.

Most concerns surrounding shale gas and tight oil development have involved environmental and human health issues, and particularly concerns over the potential risks to groundwater and surface water resources, and emissions of air pollutants, including methane. These concerns have led to calls for greater federal oversight of oil and gas development. Although primary regulatory authority over oil and natural gas exploration and production on state and private lands generally rests with the states, provisions of several federal environmental laws currently apply to certain activities associated with oil and natural gas exploration and production. Moreover, EPA is reviewing other statutory authorities and pursuing new regulatory initiatives, and BLM has proposed revisions to its oil and gas rules to specifically address hydraulic fracturing on federal and Indian lands. A broader concern, particularly from environmental groups, is that the low price of natural gas is having negative consequences for the development and growth in renewable energy sources and nuclear power, potentially resulting in another generation of greenhouse-gasproducing energy sources.

The 113th Congress has held hearings, roundtables, and other discussions on issues associated with unconventional oil and gas development broadly, and on the role of the states specifically. Bills have been introduced to expand and also to constrain federal involvement in oil and gas development involving hydraulic fracturing.

In the meantime, the Administration is pursuing actions to broaden federal oversight of this industry sector through administrative means.[77]

APPENDIX. SELECTED FEDERAL INITIATIVES RELATED TO UNCONVENTIONAL OIL AND GAS PRODUCTION

Table A-1. Selected Federal Actions Related to Unconventional Oil and Gas Production (with emphasis on hydraulic fracturing)

Agency: Statute, as Amended	Regulatory	Research	Status
EPA: Clean Air Act (CAA)	Air emissions. In 2012, EPA issued regulations that revised existing rules and promulgated new ones to regulate emissions of volatile organic compounds (VOCs), sulfur dioxide, and hazardous air pollutants (HAPs) from many production and processing activities in the oil and gas sector that had not been subject previously to federal regulation.		Rules were promulgated in August 2012 (77 Federal Register 49489); requirements phase in through 2015.
	Particularly pertinent to shale gas production are the New Source Performance Standards (NSPS), which require reductions in emissions of VOCs from hydraulically fractured natural gas wells. The rules require operators to use reduced emissions completions (green completions) for all hydraulically fractured natural gas wells beginning no later than January 2015.		EPA agreed to revisit elements of the NSPS, and on April 12, 2013, proposed revisions to the NSPS for storage tanks (78 Federal Register 22125).

Table A-1. (Continued)

Agency: Statute, as Amended	Regulatory	Research	Status
	Applying broadly across the sector, the NSPS require reductions of VOCs from compressors, pneumatic controllers, storage vessels, and other emission sources, and also revise existing standards for sulfur dioxide emissions from onshore natural gas processing plants, and HAPs from dehydrators and storage tanks.		
	In September 2013, EPA updated its 2012 performance standards for oil and natural gas to address VOC emissions from storage tanks used by the crude oil and natural gas production industry. The updates will ensure the tanks likely to have the highest emissions are controlled first, while providing tank owners and operators time to purchase and install VOC controls. The amendments reflect recent information showing that more storage tanks will be coming on line than the agency originally estimated (thus, presumably, producers need more time to purchase and install emission controls).[a]		On September 23, 2013, EPA finalized revisions to the NSPS for storage tanks (78 Federal Register 58416).

Agency: Statute, as Amended	Regulatory	Research	Status
EPA: Clean Water Act (CWA)	Wastewater discharge. Produced water and flowback from hydraulic fracturing have high levels of total dissolved solids (TDS), largely chlorides, which can harm aquatic life and affect receiving water uses (such as fishing or irrigation). EPA is updating its chloride water quality criteria for protection of aquatic life.		Draft criteria document expected in summer 2014.
	CWA Section 304(a)(1) requires EPA to develop criteria for water quality that reflect the latest scientific understanding of the effects of pollutants on aquatic life and human health. States use EPA-recommended criteria to establish state water quality standards, which in turn are used to develop enforceable discharge permits.		
	If reflected in state water quality standards, the revised chloride water quality criteria could affect discharges of produced water from extraction of conventional and unconventional oil and gas.[b]		

Table A-1. (Continued)

Agency: Statute, as Amended	Regulatory	Research	Status
EPA: CWA	Wastewater discharge. In 2011, EPA indicated that it was initiating two separate rulemakings to revise the Effluent Limitations Guidelines and Standards (ELGs) for the Oil and Gas Extraction Point Source Category to control discharges of wastewater from (1) coalbed methane (CBM) and (2) shale gas extraction. Under CWA Section 304(m), EPA sets national standards for discharges of industrial wastewater based on best available technologies that are economically achievable (BAT). States incorporate these limits into discharge permits. Shale and CBM wastewaters often contain high levels of total dissolved solids (TDS—i.e., salts), and shale gas wastewater may contain chemical contaminants, naturally occurring radioactive materials (NORM), and metals.		Notice of the final Effluent Guidelines Program Plan was published in October 2011 (76 Federal Register 66286). For shale gas wastewater, EPA plans to propose a rule in April 2014 and promulgate a final rule in December 2015.

Agency: Statute, as Amended	Regulatory	Research	Status
	Discharges to surface water: Currently, shale gas wastewater may not be discharged directly to surface waters. CBM wastewater is not subject to national discharge standards; rather, CBM wastewater discharge permits are based on best professional judgments of state or EPA permit writers. EPA was working to develop regulatory options to control direct discharges of CBM wastewaters, but determined in 2013 that no economically achievable technology was available.		Initially, EPA planned to propose a CBM rule in 2013. On August 7, 2013, EPA proposed t delist CBM from the ELG rulemaking plan based on the "declining prevalence and economic viability" of the industry. EPA determined that no economically achievable technology is available currently (78 Federal Register 48159).
	Discharges to treatment plants: current ELGs lack pretreatment standards for discharges of shale gas or CBM wastewaters to publicly owned wastewater treatment works (POTWs), which typically are not designed to treat this wastewater. EPA is developing national pretreatment standards that shale gas and CBM wastewaters would be required to meet before discharge to a POTW to ensure that the receiving facility could treat the wastewater effectively.c		

Table A-1. (Continued)

Agency: Statute, as Amended	Regulatory	Research	Status
EPA: Emergency Planning and Community Right-to-Know Act (EPCRA)	Chemical disclosure. EPA has been considering an October 2012 petition by nongovernmental organizations to subject the oil and natural gas extraction industry to Toxics Release Inventory (TRI) reporting under EPCRA. Section 313 of EPCRA requires owners or operators of certain industrial facilities to report on releases of toxic substances to the state and EPA. EPA and states are required to make nonproprietary data publicly available through the TRI website.		EPA's response to petitioners is expected in spring 2014.
EPA: Safe Drinking Water Act (SDWA)	Diesel fuels. EPA issued draft UIC Program Guidance for Permitting Hydraulic Fracturing with Diesel Fuels in response to the revised SDWA definition of "underground injection" in the Energy Policy Act (EPAct) of 2005 to explicitly exclude the underground injection of fluids (other than diesel fuels) used in hydraulic fracturing.		Draft guidance issued in May 2012. EPA submitted the guidance to the Office of Management and Budget (OMB) for review in September 2013.

Agency: Statute, as Amended	Regulatory	Research	Status
	The draft guidance provides recommendations for EPA permit writers to use in writing permits for hydraulic fracturing operations using diesel fuels. The guidance will apply in states where EPA implements the UIC program for oil and natural gas related (Class II) injection wells. States will not be required to adopt the guidance, but may do so.[d]		
EPA: SDWA		Study. EPA is studying the relationship between hydraulic fracturing and drinking water. Congress requested the study in EPA's FY2010 appropriations act. EPA designated the pending "report of results" as a "highly influential scientific assessment" (HISA), which requires peer review by qualified specialists.	Progress report issued in December 2012. During 2013 and 2014, EPA plans to issue individual reports and papers. A final report of results is expected in 2016 (extended from 2014).

Table A-1. (Continued)

Agency: Statute, as Amended	Regulatory	Research	Status
EPA: Toxic Substances Control Act (TSCA)	Chemical reporting. EPA is developing an Advance Notice of Proposed Rulemaking (ANPRM) to get input on the design and scope of possible reporting requirements for hydraulic fracturing chemicals; EPA is considering requiring information reporting under TSCA Section 8(a), and health and safety data reporting under Section 8(d).		Initiated in January 2012. Publish ANPRM in Federal Register: expected August 2014.
EPA: Resource Conservation and Recovery Act (RCRA)	Storage/disposal pits and ponds. EPA is considering developing guidance to address the design, operation, maintenance, and closure of pits used to store hydraulic fracturing fluids for reuse or pending final disposal. These wastes are exempt from regulation as a hazardous waste under RCRA.		No schedule.

Agency: Statute, as Amended	Regulatory	Research	Status
Department of the Interior, Bureau of Land Management (BLM): Mineral Leasing Act, Indian Mineral Leasing Act	Hydraulic fracturing on public lands. BLM has proposed revisions to rules governing oil and natural gas production on federal and Indian lands. BLM proposes to (1) require public disclosure of chemicals used in hydraulic fracturing, (2) tighten regulations related to well-bore integrity, and (3) add new reporting and management/storage/disposal requirements for water used in hydraulic fracturing.		Proposed in May 2012; after extensive public comment, BLM issued a Supplemental Notice of Proposed Rulemaking in May 2013. Comment period closed August 23.
Department of Homeland Security, Coast Guard: 46 U.S.C. Ch. 37	Wastewater shipment. The Coast Guard regulates the shipment of hazardous materials on the nation's rivers. Because of the potential for shale gas wastewater in the Marcellus Shale region to contain radioactive materials (especially radium, which can form surface residues and may lead to radioactive surface contamination of the barges), the Coast Guard currently does not allow barge shipment of shale gas extraction wastewater. The Coast Guard's Hazardous Materials Division has drafted a policy letter establishing requirements for bulk shipment of shale gas extraction wastewater by barge for disposal.		On October 30, 2013, the Coast Guard published a notice for a one-month comment period on a proposed policy letter setting conditions for bulk shipment of shale gas wastewater (78 Federal Register 64905).

Table A-1. (Continued)

Agency: Statute, as Amended	Regulatory	Research	Status
DOE/EPA/DOI-USGS: E.O. 13605		Federal research coordination. In 2012, the agencies agreed, through an MOU, to develop a multiagency research plan "to address the highest priority research questions associated with safely and prudently developing unconventional shale gas and tight oil resources."	Research plan was expected to be available in 2013.

Source: Prepared by the Congressional Research Service.

Notes: This table presents selected Administration activities related to unconventional oil and natural gas extraction. It excludes, for example, regional or site-specific research studies conducted by federal agencies. More information on EPA initiatives to regulate oil and gas production and hydraulic fracturing is available at EPA's website, Natural Gas Extraction—Hydraulic Fracturing, http://www2.epa.gov/hydraulicfracturing.

[a] These CAA rules, issued under court order, establish new air emissions standards for the "Crude Oil and Natural Gas Production" and "Natural Gas Transmission and Storage" source categories. For details, see CRS Report R42986, *Air Quality Issues in Natural Gas Systems: In Brief*, by Richard K. Lattanzio.

[b] For more information, see the EPA Water Quality Criteria web page, http://water swguidance/standards/criteria/.

[c] EPA explains that "[f]or direct dischargers of unconventional oil and gas wastewaters from onshore oil and gas facilities—with the exception of coalbed methane—technology-based limitations are based on the Effluent Limitations Guidelines (ELGs) for the Oil and Gas Extraction Category (40 CFR Part 435). Permits for onshore oil and gas facilities must include the requirements in Part 435, including a ban on the discharge of pollutants, except for wastewater that is of good enough quality for use in agricultural and wildlife propagation for those onshore facilities located in the continental United States and west of the 98th meridian.... Part 435 does not currently include categorical pretreatment standards for indirect discharges to publicly owned treatment works (POTWs) for wells located onshore." Source: U.S. Environmental Protection Agency, *Unconventional Extraction in the Oil and Gas Industry*, http://water wastetech/guide/oilandgas/unconv.cfm.

[d] EPA regulates the underground injection of fluids through SDWA §§1421-1426; 42 U.S.C. §§300h-300h-5. In May 2012, EPA issued draft *UIC Program Guidance for Permitting Hydraulic Fracturing with Diesel Fuels*, which generally follows EPA Class II underground injection well requirements (i.e., well construction standards; mechanical integrity testing; operating, monitoring, and reporting requirements; and public notification and financial responsibility requirements). The draft guidance provides recommendations for EPA permit writers for tailoring requirements for hydraulic fracturing using diesel fuels. The guidance will apply in states where EPA implements the UIC program for Class II wells (including Pennsylvania, New York, Michigan, Kentucky, Tennessee, and Virginia).

End Notes

[1] Hydraulic fracturing is an industry technique that uses water, sand, and chemicals under pressure to enhance the recovering of natural gas and oil. It has taken on new prominence as it has been applied to tight oil and shale gas formation as an essential method for producing resources from those types of formations.

[2] Coalbed methane and tight gas accounted for 33% of U.S. natural gas production in 2011, but are projected to account for only 28% in 2040, according to the Energy Information Administration (EIA).

[3] Full Committee Forum: Domestic Supply and Exports, Senate Energy and Natural Resources Committee, May 21, 2013, http://www.energy a3af60f7a184.

[4] "U.S. Energy Abundance: Regulatory, Market, and Legal Barriers to Export," House Energy and Commerce Committee, Subcommittee on Energy and Power, June 18, 2013, http://energycommerce.house.gov/hearing/us-energyabundance-regulatory-market-and-legal-barriers

[5] For additional information on U.S. natural gas exports, see CRS Report R42074, *U.S. Natural Gas Exports: New Opportunities, Uncertain Outcomes*, by Michael Ratner et al.

[6] For additional information on the Bakken Formation, see CRS Report R42032, *The Bakken Formation: Leading Unconventional Oil Development*, by Michael Ratner et al.

[7] For additional information on U.S. oil imports, see CRS Report R42465, *U.S. Oil Imports and Exports*, by Robert Pirog.

[8] CRS Report R41875, *The U.S.-Canada Energy Relationship: Joined at the Well*, by Paul W. Parfomak and Michael Ratner. Mexico is the third-largest source of U.S. oil imports, but is not always included in discussions of North American energy independence, as its oil sector is not as integrated with the United States as is Canada's.

[9] U.S. Energy Information Administration, *U.S. Imports of Crude Oil and Petroleum Products*, March 15, 2013, http://www.eia.gov/dnav/pet/hist/LeafHandler.ashx?n=PET

[10] Adam Sieminski, *Outlook for Shale Gas and Tight Oil Development in the U.S.*, U.S. Energy Information Administration, Presentation for the American Petroleum Institute, Washington, DC, April 4, 2013, p. 12.

[11] For a detailed discussion of environmental issues, see, for example, New York Department of Environmental Conservation, Revised Draft SGEIS on the Oil, Gas and Solution Mining Regulatory Program (September 2011): Well Permit Issuance for Horizontal Drilling and High-Volume Hydraulic Fracturing in the Marcellus Shale and Other Low-Permeability Gas Reservoirs, September 7, 2011, http://www.dec.ny.gov/energy

[12] See, for example, Amy Mall, *Incidents Where Hydraulic Fracturing is a Suspected Cause of Drinking Water Contamination*, Natural Resources Defense Council, Switchboard, updated June 17, 2013, http://switchboard.nrdc.org/ blogs/amall/incidents_where_hydraulic_frac.html.

[13] U.S. Environmental Protection Agency, *Evaluation of Impacts to Underground Sources of Drinking Water by Hydraulic Fracturing of Coalbed Methane Reservoirs*, Final Report, EPA-816-04-003, Washington, DC, June 2004, p. 4-1. (EPA reviewed 11 major coalbed methane formations to determine whether coal seams lay within underground sources of drinking water (USDWs). EPA determined that 10 of the 11 producing coal basins "definitely or likely lie entirely or partially within USDWs.")

[14] See, for example, New York State Department of Environmental Conservation, *Fact Sheet: What We Learned from Pennsylvania*, NYS DEC NEWS, http://www.dec.ny.gov/energy

[15] Department of the Interior, Environment, and Related Agencies Appropriations Act, 2010, P.L. 111-88, H.Rept. 111- 316. Drilling and fracturing methods and technologies have changed significantly over time as they have been applied to more challenging formations, greatly increasing the amount of water, fracturing fluids, and well pressures involved in oil and gas production operations. The EPA study (expected to be published in 2016) includes five case studies that involve drinking water contamination incidents in areas where unconventional oil and gas development is occurring.

[16] A 2012 Pacific Institute study found that many individuals interviewed for the study defined "hydraulic fracturing" much more broadly than the industry meaning of the term (i.e., injection of fluids into a production well). These individuals used the term broadly to include well construction, completion, and other associated activities. Noting the differences, the authors concluded that "additional work is needed to clarify terms and definitions associated with hydraulic fracturing to support more fruitful and informed dialog and to develop appropriate energy, water, and environmental policy." See *Hydraulic Fracturing and Water Resources: Separating the Frack from the Fiction*, p. 29, http://www.pacinst.org/reports/fracking/.

[17] The Marcellus Shale formation potentially represents one of the largest unconventional natural gas resources in the United States, underlying much of West Virginia and Pennsylvania, southern New York, eastern Ohio, western Maryland, and western Virginia.

[18] Katie M. Keranen, Heather M. Savage, and Geoffrey A. Abers et al., "Potentially Induced Earthquakes in Oklahoma, USA: Links between Wastewater Injection and the 2011 M_w 5.7 Earthquake Sequence," *Geology*, vol. 41, no. 3 (March 26, 2013).

[19] Such impacts may be regional or localized, and can vary seasonally or with longer-term variations in precipitation. For a discussion of water quality and supply issues associated with shale gas development, see CRS Report R42333, *Marcellus Shale Gas: Development Potential and Water Management Issues and Laws*, by Mary Tiemann et al.

[20] For a detailed discussion of air pollution issues associated with oil and gas exploration and development and recent EPA regulations, see CRS Report R42833, *Air Quality Issues in Natural Gas Systems*, by Richard K. Lattanzio.

[21] U.S. Environmental Protection Agency, *Overview of Final Amendments to Air Regulations for the Oil and Natural Gas Industry: Fact Sheet*, EPA, October 2012, http://www.epa.gov /airquality/oilandgas/pdfs/20120417fs.pdf.

[22] When vented, natural gas (largely methane) is released to the air without being burned. In contrast, when natural gas is flared (burned), the main by-product is carbon dioxide. Flaring is preferred to venting for safety reasons, but also because methane is several times more potent than carbon dioxide as a greenhouse gas (although more short-lived in the atmosphere). Flaring also reduces emissions of ozone-forming pollutants, compared to venting.

[23] See CRS Report R42032, *The Bakken Formation: Leading Unconventional Oil Development*, by Michael Ratner et al.

[24] U.S. Energy Information Administration, *Rankings: Natural Gas Marketed Production, 2011*, 2012, http://www.eia.gov/state. EIA reports gas production in 32 states and oil production in 31 states. Five states (Texas, Alaska, California, North Dakota, and Oklahoma) accounted for 56% of crude oil production in 2011, and the biggest gains were in North Dakota and Texas, due in large part to increased horizontal drilling and hydraulic fracturing activity. EIA, *Petroleum & Other Liquids*, http://www.eia.gov/dnav/pet/pet_crd_ crpdn_adc_mbbl_m.htm.

[25] The federal government, through the Bureau of Land Management (BLM), within the Department of the Interior, has responsibility for overseeing oil and gas development on federally managed lands. For a discussion of federal responsibilities for oil and gas production, see CRS Report R40806, *Energy Projects on Federal Lands: Leasing and Authorization*, by Adam Vann.

[26] States often enter into memoranda of understanding with BLM to coordinate administration and enforcement various regulatory requirements on public lands within the state.

[27] For state-specific information, see the Interstate Oil and Gas Compact Commission, *Summary of State Statutes and Regulations*, available at http://www.iogcc.state.ok.us/state-statutes

[28] See, for example, Ground Water Protection Council, U.S. Department of Energy, Office of Fossil Energy, National Energy Technology Laboratory, *State Oil and Natural Gas Regulations Designed to Protect Water Resources*, 2009, p. 24, http://www.gwpc.org/sites/default/files/state

[29] For example, before the state enacted hydraulic fracturing legislation (SB 4) in September 2013, California regulators noted that requirements for protecting underground resources and well construction standards "provide a first line of protection from potential damage caused by hydraulic fracturing." However, the state noted that "There is a gap between the requirements placed on oil and gas operators to safely construct and maintain their wells, and the information they provide to the Division about hydraulic fracturing operations and steps taken to protect resources and the environment. The Department's pending regulatory process is intended to close that gap." California Department of Conservation, *Hydraulic Fracturing in California*, http://www.conservation HydraulicFracturing.aspx. The state is currently developing regulations to implement the new law, which includes requirements for chemical disclosure, baseline and follow-up water testing for nearby water wells, notification to nearby property owners and tenants, and groundwater monitoring plans. Also, regulators are directed to make any needed revisions to rules governing construction of wells and well casings to ensure well integrity.

[30] Alabama, Arkansas, Colorado, Montana, North Dakota, New Mexico, Ohio, Pennsylvania, Texas, Utah, West Virginia, and Wyoming are among the states that have revised oil and gas rules in recent years specifically to address hydraulic fracturing. States currently revising oil and gas rules broadly include California, Indiana, Maryland, Michigan, and New York.

[31] For a comparison of state requirements for specific activities (e.g., wastewater disposal, chemical disclosure, and cementing) see Resources for the Future, *A Review of Shale Gas Regulations by State*, Center for Energy Economics and Policy, July 2012, http://www.rff.org/centers/energy

[32] General Assembly of North Carolina, Session Law 2013-365, Senate Bill 76. Also, Vermont banned hydraulic fracturing (currently, EIA does not list Vermont as an oil- or gas-producing state). The New Jersey legislature passed a ban on shale gas drilling; however, the governor vetoed the bill and imposed a one-year ban, which has expired.

[33] Jacquelyn Pless, *Natural Gas Development and Hydraulic Fracturing: a Policymaker's Guide*, National Conference of State Legislatures, June 2012, p. 5.

[34] Jacquelyn Pless, *States Take the Lead on Regulating Hydraulic Fracturing: Overview of 2012 State Legislation*, National Conference of State Legislatures, March 2013, p. 1.

[35] Ibid., pp. 2-3. North Dakota adopted a resolution urging Congress to limit EPA regulation of hydraulic fracturing. South Dakota and Utah resolutions urge Congress to clearly delegate hydraulic fracturing responsibility to the states.

[36] State requirements regarding disclosure of chemicals used in hydraulic fracturing are discussed in CRS Report R42461, *Hydraulic Fracturing: Chemical Disclosure Requirements*, by Brandon J. Murrill and Adam Vann.

[37] See, for example, Matthew McFeeley, *State Hydraulic Fracturing Disclosure Rules and Enforcement: A Comparison*, Natural Resources Defense Council, NRDC Issue Brief IB: 12-06-A, July 2012.

[38] For further discussion, see Jeffrey Logan, Garvin Heath, and Elizabeth Paranhos et al., *Natural Gas and the Transformation of the U.S. Energy Sector: Electricity*, Joint Institute for Strategic Energy Analysis, NREL/TP-6A50- 57702, Golden, CO, January 2013, http://www.nrel.gov/docs/fy13osti/55538.pdf.

[39] The 113th Congress has explored the role of states and the federal government in oil and gas production, specifically, and in environmental protection broadly. In February 2013, the House Committee on Energy and Commerce, Subcommittee on Environment and the Economy, held a hearing, *The Role of the States in Protecting the Environment Under Current Law.* The Senate Committee on Energy and Natural Resources has held a series of Natural Gas Roundtables, including a May 2013 forum on *Shale Development: Best Practices and Environmental Concerns*.

[40] For a discussion of this amendment, see CRS Report R41760, *Hydraulic Fracturing and Safe Drinking Water Act Regulatory Issues*, by Mary Tiemann and Adam Vann.

[41] CWA Section 301 prohibits the discharge of pollutants into the nation's waters except in compliance with the provisions of the law, which include obtaining a discharge permit. 33 U.S.C. §1311. For information on applicable CWA requirements, see Environmental Protection Agency, "Natural Gas Drilling in the Marcellus Shale, NPDES Program Frequently Asked Questions," March 16, 2011, http://www.epa.gov/npdes/pubs/hydro fracturing_faq.pdf.

[42] The Safe Drinking Water Act of 1974 (P.L. 93-523) authorized the Underground Injection Control (UIC) program at EPA. UIC provisions, as amended, are contained in SDWA Part C, §§1421-1426; 42 U.S.C. §§300h-300h-5.

[43] EPAct 2005 (P.L. 109-58, §322), amended SDWA to exempt from the definition of underground injection the injection of fluids or propping agents (other than diesel fuel) for hydraulic fracturing purposes.

[44] The rules regulate VOC emissions from hydraulically fractured natural gas wells, compressors, pneumatic controllers, storage vessels, and leaking components at onshore natural gas processing plants, as well as sulfur dioxide emissions from onshore natural gas processing plants. The new standards require producers to capture about 90% of the natural gas that escapes into the atmosphere as a result of production using hydraulic fracturing. For further discussion, see CRS Report R42986, *Air Quality Issues in Natural Gas Systems: In Brief*, by Richard K. Lattanzio.

[45] For details, see CRS Report R43152, *Hydraulic Fracturing: Selected Legal Issues*, by Adam Vann, Brandon J. Murrill, and Mary Tiemann.

[46] The Department of the Interior, Environment, and Related Agencies Appropriations Act, 2010 (P.L. 111-88, H.Rept. 111-316):

Hydraulic Fracturing Study.—The conferees urge the Agency to carry out a study on the relationship between hydraulic fracturing and drinking water, using a credible approach that relies on the best available science, as well as independent sources of information. The conferees expect the study to be conducted through a transparent, peer-reviewed process that will ensure the validity and accuracy of the data. The Agency shall consult with other Federal agencies as well as appropriate State and interstate regulatory agencies in carrying out the study, which should be prepared in accordance with the Agency's quality assurance principles.

[47] U.S. Environmental Protection Agency, *Plan to Study the Potential Impacts of Hydraulic Fracturing on Drinking Water Sources*, Office of Research and Development, EPA/600/R-11/122, November 2011.

[48] EPA is conducting retrospective case studies at five sites to develop information about the potential impacts of hydraulic fracturing on drinking water resources under different circumstances. The case studies include (1) the Bakken Shale in Dunn County, ND; (2) the Barnett Shale in Wise County, TX; (3) the Marcellus Shale in Bradford County, PA; (4) the Marcellus Shale in Washington County, PA; and (5) coalbed methane in the Raton Basin, CO.

[49] U.S. Environmental Protection Agency, *Study of the Potential Impacts of Hydraulic Fracturing on Drinking Water Resources: Progress Report*, Office of Research and Development, EPA 601/R-12/011, December 2012, http://www2.epa.gov/hfstudy/study.

[50] Ibid., p. 6.

[51] Because EPA has designated the "report of results" as a "highly influential scientific assessment," the agency is to follow the peer review planning requirements described in the Office of Management and Budget's *Information Quality Bulletin for Peer Review*, 2004. The Bulletin states that important scientific information must be peer reviewed by qualified specialists before being disseminated by the federal government. The EPA Science Advisory Board is an external federal advisory committee that conducts peer reviews of significant EPA research products and activities.

[52] The White House, "Blueprint for a Secure Energy Future," March 30, 2011, p. 13, http://www.whitehouse.gov/sites/ default/files/blueprint_secure_energy_future.pdf.

[53] U.S. Department of Energy, the Secretary of Energy Advisory Board (SEAB), Shale Gas Production Subcommittee, *Second Ninety Day Report*, November 18, 2011, http://www.shalegas.energy.gov/. In November 2013, Secretary Moniz requested the SEAB to form a task force to review how FracFocus "houses the information Federal and State regulatory agencies require as part of their regulatory functions with regard to disclosure of the composition and quantities of fracturing fluids injected into unconventional oil and gas wells." This review is under way.

[54] Executive Order 13605, "Supporting Safe and Responsible Development of Unconventional Domestic Natural Gas Resources," (Washington: GPO, 2012), http://www.gpo.gov/fdsys /pkg/DCPD-201200269/pdf/DCPD-201200269.pdf.

[55] The Memorandum of Agreement is available at the Administration website, Multi-Agency Collaboration on Unconventional Oil and Gas Research, http://unconventional.energy

[56] Mineral Leasing Act of 1920, 30 U.S.C. §181.

[57] For a discussion of federal lands leasing authorities and activities, see CRS Report R40806, *Energy Projects on Federal Lands: Leasing and Authorization*, by Adam Vann.

[58] 77 *Federal Register* 27691-27693.

[59] Department of the Interior, Bureau of Land Management, "Oil and Gas; Well Stimulation, Including Hydraulic Fracturing, on Federal and Indian Lands," 77 *Federal Register* 27691, May 11, 2012.

[60] The proposed rule would amend existing BLM regulations at 43 C.F.R. Section 316.3-2.

[61] 77 *Federal Register* 27692-27693.

[62] Department of the Interior, Bureau of Land Management, "Oil and Gas; Hydraulic Fracturing on Federal and Indian Lands: Supplemental Notice of Proposed Rulemaking," 78 *Federal Register* 31636, May 24, 2013.

[63] SNPR, §3162.3-3(a) and §3160.0-5. This revision excludes acidizing, enhanced secondary and tertiary recovery so that the rule would apply only to hydraulic fracturing and not to other "well stimulation" activities.

[64] SNPR, §3162.3-3(k). In 2012, BLM proposed to implement on public lands "whichever rules, state or Federal, are most protective of Federal lands and resources and the environment, consistent with longstanding practice and relevant statutory authorities." 77 *Federal Register* 72694.

[65] SNPR, §3162.3-3(i). Operators submitting information through FracFocus would be required to certify that the information is correct and certify that the operator complied with applicable laws governing notice and permits.

[66] SNPR, §3162.3-3(j)1-4. Modeled on Colorado rules, BLM would instruct operators not to disclose trade secret information to BLM or on FracFocus. Operators would submit an affidavit stating that withheld information is entitled to withholding. BLM would retain authority to require operators to submit claimed trade secret information.

[67] SNPR, §3162.3-3(f).

[68] SNPR, §3162.3-3(b) and §3162.3-3(d).

[69] SNPR, §3162.3-3(d).

[70] This action is based on authority in 46 U.S.C. Chapter 37—"Carriage of Liquid Bulk Dangerous Cargoes." Implementing regulations are published in 46 C.F.R. Subchapter O—"Certain Bulk Dangerous Cargoes."

[71] See 46 C.F.R. 153.900(c)-(d) or 46 C.F.R. 151.01-15.

[72] U.S. Coast Guard, *Marine Safety Engineering, Shale Gas Extraction Waste Water*, Commercial Regulations and Standards Directorate, Fall 2012, p. 5, http://www.uscg.mil/hq/cg5/cg52/docs/2012fall.pdf.

[73] Department of Homeland Security, Coast Guard, "Carriage of Conditionally Permitted Shale Gas Extraction Waste Water in Bulk: Notice of Availability and Request for Comments," 78 *Federal Register* 64905, October 30, 2013.

[74] Similar bills were offered in the 112th Congress, but none was enacted. H.R. 1084/S. 587 proposed repealing the hydraulic fracturing exemption established in the Energy Policy Act (EPAct) of 2005, and amending the term "underground injection" to include the injection of fluids used in hydraulic fracturing operations, thus authorizing EPA to regulate this process under the SDWA. The bills also would have required disclosure of the chemicals used in the fracturing process. In response to rules proposed by BLM in 2012, S. 2248/H.R. 4322 proposed that a state would have sole authority to regulate hydraulic fracturing on federal lands within state boundaries; H.R. 3973 would have prohibited the rule from having any effect on Indian lands; and H.R. 6235 would have barred a final rule for 10 years, pending an impact study.

For further discussion, see CRS Report R41760, *Hydraulic Fracturing and Safe Drinking Water Act Regulatory Issues*, by Mary Tiemann and Adam Vann.

[75] 30 U.S.C. §181 et seq.

[76] 42 U.S.C. §300h-4.

[77] See the Appendix for a review of federal research and regulatory initiatives related to unconventional oil and gas production, with emphasis on hydraulic fracturing.

INDEX

C

D

E

F

G

H

M

N

O

P

Q

R

S

T

U

V

W